Grand Canyon

Other books by
Joseph Wood Krutch

available from
The University of Arizona Press

The Desert Year

*The Forgotten Peninsula:
A Naturalist in Baja California*

Grand Canyon

Today and All Its Yesterdays

Joseph Wood Krutch

The University of Arizona Press

Tucson

*To Marcelle, who always shared even
the solitudes of the Canyon with me.*

Copyright © 1957, 1958 by Joseph Wood Krutch
All Rights Reserved
THE UNIVERSITY OF ARIZONA PRESS

Copyright © 1989
The Arizona Board of Regents
Manufactured in the United States of America
Published by arrangement with William Morrow & Company, Inc.
⊗ This book is printed on acid-free, archival-quality paper.
93 92 91 90 89   5 4 3 2 1

Portions of this book have appeared in *The New York Times Magazine* and in *American
Forests*.
Grateful acknowledgment is made to Houghton Mifflin Company for permission to
quote from *A Thousand Mile Walk to the Gulf*, by John Muir, and to the Department
of the Interior for permission to reproduce the map appearing on pages viii–ix, and
the cross section on pages 36–37.

Library of Congress Cataloging-in-Publication Data

Krutch, Joseph Wood, 1893–1970.
    Grand Canyon: today and all its yesterdays / Joseph Wood Krutch.
        p. cm.
    Reprint. Originally published: New York: W. Sloan Associates,
1958.
    ISBN 0-8165-1112-8 (alk. paper)
    1. Grand Canyon (Ariz.)—Description and travel. 2. Grand Canyon
(Ariz.)—History. 3. Krutch, Joseph Wood, 1893–1970—Journeys—
Arizona—Grand Canyon. I. Title.
F788.K88 1989   89-33054
979.1'32—dc20   CIP

British Library Cataloguing in Publication data are available.

"The finest workers in stone are not copper or steel tools, but the gentle touches of air and water working at their leisure with a liberal allowance of time."

Thoreau

The author wishes to thank Edwin D. McKee of the U.S. Geological Survey for reading Chapters II, III, IV and V, and Louis Schellbach, formerly Chief Naturalist at Grand Canyon National Park, for reading the entire Ms. He received valuable suggestions and criticisms from both but neither is, of course, responsible for any of the statements made. To Mrs. George Voevodsky and Mrs. Hubert d'Autremont he is grateful for charming company on two different jaunts to the Canyon and thereabouts.

The terms "Archean" and "Algonkian" are no longer part of the official geological terminology but are used here because they are those employed in most of the existing literature to which a reader may be led.

A few paragraphs from Chapter II have appeared in "The American Scholar" and portions of Chapters I and XIV in, respectively, "The New York Times Magazine" and "American Forests." The author extends thanks to the editors of these publications for permission to reprint the material.

Contents

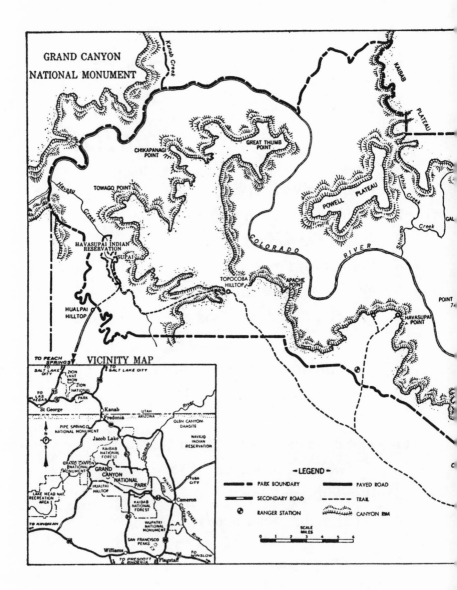

GRAND CANYON NATIONAL PARK
ARIZONA

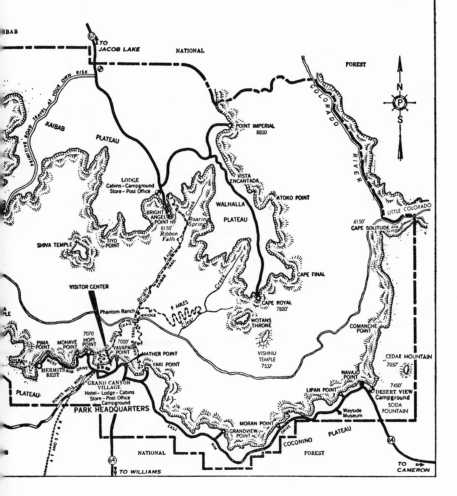

Grand Canyon

1

Where solitude is easy to find

Twenty years ago I was one of the tourist thousands who saw Grand Canyon for the first time. In those days, travelers approaching from the south by car or bus had no warning until they stood actually upon the brink. Usually they descended at the front door of Bright Angel Lodge, passed through the lobby, and wandered across the terrace at the other side, wondering as they went where the Canyon was. Then, suddenly, they were at the brink with only a low parapet between them and a vast abyss.

First there is the sheer drop of several thousand feet, then the wide Tonto Plateau, then another sheer drop to an invisible bottom whose depth the visitor can only guess. Apparently this was the way Cárdenas, the first white man to see the Canyon, came upon it in 1540. Since then thousands of men and women have shared his wonder and delight. Though I have made many visits since my first, I still get a real if diminished shock.

Today a new road, built only a few years ago, gives automobilists a glimpse into the chasm as they approach. That spoils a bit of the drama; but perhaps it is just as well. On my first visit a fellow traveler took one look and then ran back to throw his arms around a tree. When I saw him last, he was desperately resisting the efforts of two women companions to pry him loose.

At first glance the spectacle seems too strange to be real. Because one has never seen anything like it, because one has nothing to compare it with, it stuns the eye but cannot really hold the attention. For one thing, the scale is too large to be credited. The Canyon is ten miles across from rim to rim at the point where one usually sees it first and almost exactly a mile deep. But we are so accustomed to thinking of skyscrapers as high and of St. Peter's or the Pentagon as massive that we can hardly help misinterpreting what the eye sees; we cannot realize that the tremendous mesas and curiously shaped buttes which rise all around us are the grandiose objects they are. For a time it is too much like a scale model or an optical illusion. One admires the peep show and that is all. Because we cannot relate our-

Where solitude is easy to find

selves to it, we remain outside, very much as we remain outside the frame of a picture. And though we may come back to a picture again and again, we cannot look at it continuously for any considerable period of time. To pass on to another picture is the almost inevitable impulse. And this is the reaction of a majority of visitors to the Canyon.

To get into the picture one must relate one's self to it somehow and that is not easy to do in a short time. A few of the more hardy take the daylong journey on muleback to the bottom and return. A few of the more foolhardy brush warnings aside and plunge gaily downward on foot only to discover—unless they are seasoned hikers—that they have to be rescued in a state of exhaustion from an illusory panorama through which, as in a dream, they seem unable to make any progress. They have related themselves, but the relation is one of frustration and defeat.

A more sensible procedure for those willing to take the time is to allow the relationship to establish itself gradually. After a few days well but quietly spent, one begins to lose the sense of unreality and to come to terms with a scale of magnitude and of distance which could not at first be taken in. And it is only then that the spectacle, even as mere spectacle, makes its full impression or that one begins to have some dim sense of what the geologists mean when they talk of the millions of years during which the Canyon was cut and of the billions during which the rocks were prepared for the cutting. The Canyon requires what we call in the lingo of our day "a double take." Only that way does its size, its antiquity or the grandioseness of the forces which made it become real. Moreover, as I have learned from many visits, the process has to be repeated every time. First there is the impression of some sort of man-made diorama trying to fool the eye. Only later comes the gradual acceptance of the unbelievable fact.

Hendrik van Loon once remarked—I have not checked his figures—that the entire human population of the earth could be packed in a box only a mile wide, deep, and high. He then went on to add that if such a box were dropped into the middle of Grand Canyon, it would just about reach the rim but be not much more conspicuous than many of the mesas which here and there rise almost as high. Only a confirmed misanthropist will feel that the experiment would be worth making, but the visitor is soon struck by a more benign demonstration. This is that men—even hordes of men —cannot fill the Canyon sufficiently to detract from the sense of vast emptiness.

This is, after all, one of the most visited spots on the face of the earth. As the Swiss hotel is said to have boasted, "Thousands come here from all parts of the world seeking solitude." But at Grand Canyon at least they can find it. They form their little knot, of course, around the hotel and its terrace. But one can lose them very easily and then literally have a whole landscape to oneself. Even from the terrace of Bright Angel Lodge the Canyon itself is so empty that a little flurry of excitement arises when someone spots through

Where solitude is easy to find

his binoculars a speck moving up the side or across a plateau and when it can be assumed, though not actually seen, that the speck is a man or perhaps a man and a mule. The rim itself, except for the short stretch on either side of the main tourist area, is equally deserted. A few miles away—indeed within easy walking distance—one finds without looking a hundred perches where one may sit in absolute solitude, looking across a vista of many miles in which there is neither a human being nor any sign that any human being was ever there. And it is from such a perch that those who wish to take the Canyon in should begin to make its acquaintance.

Actually, of course, there are many areas in the Southwest a great deal farther from the conveniences and inconveniences of civilization—places hundreds of miles from a railroad and scores from a paved or even graded road; places where no man may come for months or even years. One knows that this is so and when one visits such a region the knowledge has its effect upon the imagination. But I cannot say that I ever looked upon any scene which, on the basis of what the eye could see, appeared to be more completely out of the world of man and modernity, although actually my perch was perhaps half a mile from a paved highway along which cars were passing at the rate of a hundred an hour, and only two or three miles from a crowded resort hotel. It is a pity—or perhaps it isn't—that so few visitors realize how close they are to an experience not elsewhere easy to have in the twentieth century, and the fact that one can have it so easily here reminds one again of the scale of this landscape. If, as Mr. van Loon said, the entire population of the earth could be all but lost in the Canyon, it is no wonder that a few thousands leave lots of unoccupied space.

Not very long ago, and after an absence of several years, I again took up my position on one of the little promontories which jut out from the rim. It was past the middle of June, and in the thin air of seven thousand feet even visitors from the southern Arizona desert are burned one tone deeper. But in the shade of a piñon pine the air still hints of the nights which can be almost cold, even at that season.

I looked across the ten miles to the opposite rim, down the successive terraces to the inner gorge at whose invisible bottom the great river still runs after having cut through a mile of stone, and then at the wall of an opposite promontory on my own side. I checked where I could the dividing lines between the successive formations of the geological ages—the Permian limestone on which I sat, the hundreds of feet of sandstone below it, the great Redwall of the Carboniferous age, the resisting plateau of Cambrian sediments, and finally the black wall of Archean schist. I made, in other words, a brief attempt at adjustment to the world of time as well as of space. But for the moment I was less interested in what the Canyon had been than in what it is at this moment and has been able to remain. It is not often that twentieth-century man has so much space to himself.

Here and there near the rim and below its edge there are scattered evidences that Indians inhabited the area—as one tribe still inhabits a section of the Canyon itself. But no evi-

Where solitude is easy to find

dence of even long past occupation was visible from where
I sat, and indeed it nowhere appears that many men ever
lived very long or very well here. This is dry country with
thin soil or none, and also, perhaps, as one may at least
fancy, a little too disconcerting in the immensities of its
vistas. Yet it is by no means lifeless and now, as in the past,
various small creatures find it very much to their liking.
Violet green swallows dip and swerve, now above, now below the rim. Ravens soar above, nonchalantly putting another few hundred feet between them and the bottom a
mile below where I sit. And if they seem to take the abyss
with the casualness inspired by confidence in their strong
wings and the solidity of the air for those who know how to
navigate it, there are many other creatures obviously un-
aware of the terrible chasm open at their feet. Chipmunks
and rock squirrels scamper a few feet below the edge; lizards dart here and there; a small gopher snake, apparently
stalking some game, wiggles slowly across a piece of crum-
bling stone which a slight push would send hurtling below.
Little junipers anchored at the very edge dangle bare roots
over the side. And there, two feet below the rim, a pentste-
mon waves a red wand over nothingness.

Despite all these living things so obviously at home here,
there is absolutely no sign from which I would be able to deduce that any man besides myself had ever been here or,
for that matter, that he had ever existed at all. This scene, I
say to myself, would be exactly what it is if he never had. It
is not quite the world before man came, because too many

other living things have disappeared since then. But otherwise it is still the world as though man had never been.

At least there is absolutely nothing to remind me of all that he has done in (and to) the globe he lives on. The tamer of fire and the inventor of the wheel might never have existed—to say nothing of Newton and Watt and Faraday. Neither is there anything to remind me of the less dubious human achievements with which I have been concerned for most of my life. Plato and Shakespeare and Mozart also might never have existed, and if I had never come in contact with anything not visible here, I can hardly imagine what my life would have been like or what the character of my consciousness would be.

Here, so I am tempted to say, are the eternal hills without the eternal thoughts with which we have clothed them. Yet actually the hills are not eternal, whether the thoughts are or are not. In half a dozen places I can see the still visible evidences of recent rockfalls where great slabs of stone have broken loose and gone hurtling down. The widening of the Canyon is going on visibly, its deepening invisibly and no doubt much more slowly. One does not have to think in terms of geological time to realize that even the Canyon is changing. It is wider than it was a century ago and will inevitably be wider still after another has passed.

Man changes the face of the earth much more rapidly than nature does and he is creeping up on this area. Just out of sight are the tumbled-down remains of a miner's cabin.

Where solitude is easy to find

The miner came, scratched the surface a little and dug a few insignificant holes. Then he and the others like him admitted defeat, though this one has left a name and a bit of a legend behind him.

> They say the Lion and the Lizard keep
> The Courts where Jamshyd gloried and drank deep. . . .

Well, I don't know how much John Hance gloried or how deep he drank. I do know that the mountain lion does not keep court there because the lion has been all but exterminated in the area and his extermination has not been an unmixed blessing, even for man. But the lizard eludes us, and when I visited Hance's cabin a few minutes before taking up my perch, a lizard was sunning himself on the sagging door Hance had built for himself.

Modern man will not give up so easily. Scarcely a mile from where I sat a paved road was carrying cars to a village from which telegraph and telephone reach out. Magazines and newspapers are delivered. Occasionally an airplane hurtling across the continent passes overhead. A year or two ago two of them collided improbably above the Canyon and fell into its depths. These—or at least some of them—are good things to have but not unmitigated comforts. They suggest by what a narrow margin (and possibly for how short a time) such primitive, isolated spots as my perch may continue to exist.

How many more generations will pass before it will have become nearly impossible to be alone even for an hour, to

GRAND CANYON

see anywhere nature as she is without man's improvements upon her? How long will it be before—what is perhaps worse yet—there is no quietness anywhere, no escape from the rumble and the crash, the clank and the screech which seem to be the inevitable accompaniment of technology? Whatever man does or produces, noise seems to be an unavoidable by-product. Perhaps he can, as he now tends to believe, do anything. But he cannot do it quietly.

Perhaps when the time comes that there is no more silence and no more aloneness, there will also be no longer anyone who wants to be alone. If man is the limitlessly conditionable creature so many believe him to be, then inevitably the desire for a thing must disappear when it has become no longer attainable. Even now fewer and fewer are *aware* of any desire to escape from crowds, and most men and women who still make traditional excursions to beach or picnic grounds unpack their radios without delay and turn on a noise to which they do not listen. But it is not certain that this is not a morbid appetite rather than one which has become normal or that it, any more than any other morbid appetite, brings real satisfaction when it is gratified.

There is also another aspect to the situation. At least a few do still consciously seek quietness and some degree of solitude; a great many more seek it less consciously, but seek it nonetheless. If this were not so, the various national parks would not be so persistently visited. When all possible discount has been allowed for the irrelevant motives, for the frequent failure to get what the visitor presumably came for,

Where solitude is easy to find

and for the perverseness of many who try to avoid the very things which the parks have to offer, the fact still remains that many find (and many others do not find only because they do not know how to find it) that brief experience with solitude, silence, and a glimpse of nature herself which, to some greater or less degree, they do feel the need of.

As a matter of fact, the deliberate search for them is a modern phenomenon not, I think, because they were never before enjoyed but because they were taken for granted. Only when they began to be scarce, only after the natural rather than the man-made, and solitude rather than company had to be sought after, did the great empty spaces become attractive or, indeed, other than alarming. Man's place in nature was precarious long before the situation was reversed and it became nature rather than man whose survival seemed uncertain.

If the first white man ever to see the Canyon felt anything except frustration when he came upon this great barrier he saw no hope of crossing, his journal gives no hint of the fact. Cárdenas had been dispatched by Coronado on a side trip in order to scout out a part of the region where they were searching for the seven Golden Cities that did not exist, and Cárdenas was in no mood to look at scenery or to indulge the luxury of wonder. He had had more than enough of empty, inhospitable spaces. He had had hardships and "adventures" aplenty. He had made almost impossible journeys overcoming almost unconquerable impediments. And here was a difficulty which could not be overcome. He had been led on and on in the hope that the difficulties were almost over. Now, after all he had gone through, nature laughed and said, "Thus far shalt thou go and no farther." In his day even the Alps were still regarded almost universally as "horrid"—a barrier to be dreaded before one came upon it and to be looked back upon with shuddering after it had been conquered.

The white men known to have seen the Canyon during the next three centuries can be counted on the fingers of one hand. And when in 1857 Lieutenant Joseph C. Ives made for the United States Government an extensive reconnaissance in the region of its western end, he wrote in his report: "Ours has been the first and will doubtless be the last party of whites to visit this profitless locality. It seems intended by nature that the Colorado river, along the greater portion of its lonely and majestic way, shall be forever unvisited and undisturbed."

Forgivable, perhaps, since Lieutenant Ives could hardly be expected to know either how transportation would increase the mobility of men or, what is perhaps more important, that the America which was even in his day still largely wilderness, was so soon to become the America in which wilderness is a rarity.

Forgivable or not, this was certainly one of the unluckiest prophecies ever made, and Ives would be hardly less astonished than Cárdenas to be told that this region "destined to be forever unvisited and undisturbed" is actually

Where solitude is easy to find

one of the most frequently visited on earth—at least if one uses the word "visited" to mean sought out purely in order to be looked at. Yet two of the words he used do nevertheless suggest the beginning of the change in man's attitude toward the more grandiose and least conquerable aspects of the natural world. Cárdenas would not have spoken of the Colorado as "majestic." That word could have been used only by a man upon whose sensibilities a new attitude had already taken some effect. Ives was echoing the changed language of Europeans to whom "horrid mountains" had become "awful mountains" and the once merely terrifying had become "sublime." Three centuries had been required to change Cárdenas' dismay into the reaction which Ives revealed not only in the word "majestic" but almost equally in the word "lonely," which is already touched with a romantic aura. Hardly more than half a century later this area destined to be "forever unvisited" was a national park preserved for its own "awful" sake.

Another change equally significant in its different way is evident in the report of a scientific member of the Ives party. Cárdenas had no curiosity concerning the origin or meaning of the Canyon. He would never have asked (or cared) what could be learned from it about the history of the earth. He would have liked to be able to get to the other side and he would have liked to get there only because gold might be found there. At least that would have been the only reason he could have given, though one may guess that the desire for gold, like its companion motive, the desire to save Indian souls, may have sometimes been partly a rationalization of the desire for adventure. Such a desire seemed less readily understandable then than now, because one did not then have to go as far as one has to go today to find novel and testing experiences. John S. Newberry, who was Ives' geologist, had on the other hand the advantage of living in an age when one could ask and get some answer to the question "What does this Canyon mean?" and he sketched out a broadly accurate account of the Canyon's geological significance.

By 1890, C. Hart Merriam, who made for the Department of Agriculture the first "Biological Survey of the San Francisco Region and Desert of the Little Colorado, Arizona" could state the third reason why the Canyon repays study—namely that it is a self-contained biological unit. "In short," so he wrote, "the Grand Canyon of the Colorado is a world in itself, and a great fund of knowledge is in store for the philosophic biologist whose privilege it is to study exhaustively the problems there presented."

On my own first visit twenty years ago I think I had no more definite idea of what had brought me, no more knowledge of the various kinds of things which the Canyon region is and has to offer, than the average tourist. To me also it was then little more than "spectacle," one of "the wonders of the world" which one feels some vague obligation to see and gets some vague pride out of having seen. Like everybody else, I took a few pictures and probably dispatched a few post cards. Then I departed, taking little more with me than what a post card will hold.

I did not then recognize more than very dimly the need or the desire for that experience of a world we did not make which was later to become so important to me. Neither was I aware of more than a very casual interest in what is known about the way in which the Canyon was made or what it reveals of time and history. Yet there was just enough recognition of the one and interest in the other to bring me back. And even for those whose attitude is still what mine then was, a *part* of the half-understood fascination is the result of a vaguely perceived sense that the spectacle represents something the imagination could feed upon and that it is ready to tell a story to those who will listen.

What I hope to write about in this book is both what it has meant to the imagination and what I have learned about its uniquely revealing history of our earth. The Canyon is at least two things besides spectacle. It is a biological unit and the most revealing single page of earth's history anywhere open on the face of the globe.

2

Water doesn't run uphill

Those who write about the Canyon generally begin by saying that it is indescribable; then they undertake to describe it. That error, at least, I shall attempt to avoid. Few have not seen some of the innumerable photographs which have been taken from hundreds of different points of view and, inadequate as they necessarily are, they give a better notion of the superficial features than direct word pictures can. They hardly suggest the vastness of the scale, but statistics also mean little because the imagination does not take them in.

19

Water doesn't run uphill

You can say that the winding course of the Canyon is more than two hundred miles long, that it varies from four to eighteen miles in breadth, and that the walls of the inner gorge are, in most places, so steep that it is impossible to climb out—as various early adventurers discovered too late when their boats were wrecked and they left their skeletons in a prison from which they had not been able to escape. You can add that between Navajo Bridge, near the eastern entrance to the Canyon, and Lake Mead—which is two hundred miles by river to the west—the only place where it can be crossed by tourists is the little foot-and-mule bridge a vertical mile below the point where the two hotels face one another across a ten-mile gap. You can add that the shortest way to get across that ten-mile gap without making the arduous journey down one side and up the other is to make the more than two-hundred-mile journey which carries you around the eastern end of the Canyon and then west and south to the point just opposite the one you left.

Finally, if you like to go in for superlatives, you can say that no other valley (and a canyon is simply a narrow valley) is at once so deep and so narrow; that though there are narrower gorges and, in the Alps, for example, wider valleys lying farther below the summits of the mountains enclosing them, there is nowhere else on earth a valley or canyon at once so deep, so long, and so closely hemmed in by its walls. This last is the simplest and most obvious of the facts which make Grand Canyon seem unique even at first glance. But perhaps the wisest thing to say about it is

GRAND CANYON

what the distinguished German geologist, Hans Cloos, tells us: "I remembered, or tried to remember, that the Rhine Valley at Caub is only a few hundred yards wide and deep, and yet is also called a 'canyon.'"

Seen only from the rim and thought of only as a spectacle, the "view" has some of the insubstantiality of a cloudscape changing color and form almost from moment to moment. By noon the reds and whites and greens have been faded out to pastel shades, and the bold contours flattened almost to two dimensions. Then, as the sun moves westward and shadows begin to form, the strong colors begin to stand out again, the massive mesas and buttes which had been flattened against the opposite wall until they were almost unnoticed step boldly forth, and all the innumerable minor terraces, side canyons, and pointed projections emerge in sharp relief. In late afternoon the depths begin to fill with a haze which looks almost like sea fog but is actually blue sky, or at least the result of the same phenomena which make the sky seem blue—namely, sunlight scattered by innumerable tiny particles in a very dry and almost dust-free air. As the sun sets, its red light gives a fiery glow to the red sandstone and shale which form the eminences lifted out of the mist.

The tradition that has been followed in naming the various mesas and buttes "Shiva Temple," "Vishnu Temple," etc. is perhaps regrettable. It prettifies and trivializes what it might be better to leave without the distracting element of

Water doesn't run uphill

inadequate comparison. These "temples" are much larger and much more ancient than any historical names can suggest. Nevertheless, the tradition was begun in Major Powell's time and has at least the justification that if these great monuments are to be compared with anything man-made, it is the Oriental they suggest. They are not Gothic and they are even more obviously not Classic. But they do seem to suggest the riotous fancy of the East and have reminded many a spectator of the Angkor Vat—though neither any Oriental potentate nor even any Egyptian Pharaoh ever dared dream of construction on such a scale. By comparison, the largest pyramid is a pimple on the face of the earth.

Here we come face to face with one of the greatest paradoxes of the Canyon. It looks lawless, fantastic and whimsical. If it were on a lesser scale, one would be tempted to say "freakish." By comparison with the great simple outlines of most of nature's great works, by comparison with the Alps or the Himalayas or even Yosemite and Lake Louise, it seems deficient in rhyme or reason; a curiosity or mere anomaly; something dreamed rather than something illustrative of the grand principles in accordance with which our globe was formed.

Actually, however, once one has begun to grasp its meaning in structural terms, its rationale begins to emerge, and one begins to understand it, not as cloudscape, but as an astounding demonstration of what can happen when the same great forces that have elsewhere sculptured the earth in such varied but oft repeated ways worked out their problem under a set of conditions never met elsewhere on any such scale.

Every feature expresses that logic which we have come to find indispensable in the human architecture we most admire. For every feature there is a why and a wherefore. And the plain answers to the why, the clearness of the logic, are the reasons for both its uniqueness and the sustained interest it can arouse. Nowhere else are landscape and geology more intimately related; the one more clearly an expression of the other. But the logic is not immediately apparent.

A tale often told in various versions concerns a cowboy (or a prospector or a scout) who found himself suddenly upon the rim, who gasped, and then exclaimed aloud: "Something has happened here!" Obviously something has—something stupendous and seemingly catastrophic. From the days of the Indians who wandered in and around it, through the days of the legendary cowboy and down to those of the real tourist, explanations ranging from the moderately ingenious to the howlingly absurd have been given.

Like so many peoples in so many different parts of the world, the Navajos have a flood story, and according to them a great inland sea at one time covered the whole area round about until finally it broke a passageway through the canyon and then ran out. Since there was no Navajo Noah, all their ancestors were turned into fish. For that reason no good Navajo will eat fish—except, perhaps, out of a can of trader's

Water doesn't run uphill

salmon from which the label has been removed. And before you ask him how *he* happens to be here if all his fore-fathers became fish, just pause to consider that he might, if he has been to an Indian Agency school, ask you in return, who Cain's wife was. In religious discussions such questions are bad manners.

More sophisticated answers offer a wide choice though most of them will not stand up under even moderately search-ing examination. Perhaps, so it has been said, the Canyon is a great crack which broke open when the earth cooled—a simple theory very attractive to those who imagine that we are living directly upon the cooled crust of a once molten ball. But it is a theory hardly tenable in view of the fact that thousands of fossils lie buried in the Canyon walls and could not very well have been laid down there while the earth was hot.

Still more fantastic was the suggestion that the Colorado was once an underground river flowing through a cavern whose ceiling fell in; somewhat more ingenious is the theory that, since the promontories of the two rims could be more or less exactly fitted into one another, they drifted apart, leaving the gap through which the river might flow. After all, there is a respectable geological theory that Africa and South America, which do look like adjacent parts of a jig-saw puzzle, were once joined. And one of the projects of the Geophysical Year was to attempt to determine whether or not any "continental drift" is now detectable.

The simplest, most inclusive and at the same time vaguest

explanation is that which eighteenth-century geologists gave when faced with any great disturbance of the earth's crust: "cataclysm," or "catastrophe," they said. Or, in the cowboy's words, "something happened"—something sudden, violent and too explosive to be reasoned about. That, in the day of Cuvier and before Lyell founded modern geology, was the answer to everything. From time to time, it was assumed, the earth heaved, broke, and in the ensuing chaos every living thing was destroyed so that, once things had quieted down again, life had to start all over again, experimenting after each catastrophe with new forms until, sometime after the most recent, the Garden of Eden was planted and all the plants and animals now living (including, of course, man) were created. Hardly more than a century and a half ago that was what most people who had thought at all about such matters believed. The theory had, moreover, at least a secondary convenience. It accounted for the obviously very ancient fossils as vestiges of previous creations and made it possible to believe that man and all the still living animals were created on the sixth day of a recent new beginning.

If you listen long enough by the parapet in front of Bright Angel Lodge, you will hear all these theories expounded. But there is also a whole class of new ones which would never have occurred to the men of any age before ours and which reveal a fundamental change in man's sense of the relation between nature's powers and his: those explanations, I mean, which suggest human agency.

Water doesn't run uphill

One park ranger insists that he was asked some years ago if the Canyon had been a WPA project. Perhaps the propounder of this question was only a satiric rogue. But suggestions almost as preposterous have been seriously made, and they are usually introduced with some such remark as, "You can't tell me it was made without human aid." Probably I should find it impossible to believe that any of the "human aid" theories were seriously advanced had I not myself once been stunned into silence by an educated woman who would hear no objections to her firm conviction that the vast sandstone buttes in Monument Valley were the remains of an ancient civilization.

Behind all such suggestions lies the unconscious assumption that man's works are by now the most imposing on earth and that his power now exceeds nature's. No age before ours would have made such an assumption. Man has always before thought of himself as puny by comparison with natural forces, and he was humble before them. But we have been so impressed by the achievements of technology that we are likely to think we can do more than nature herself. We dug the Panama Canal, didn't we? Why not the Grand Canyon? Actually we are suffering from delusions of grandeur, from a state of hubris which may bring about a tragic catastrophe in the end. And I cannot imagine how we may be cured of it if the only effect of coming face to face with the most impressive demonstrations of what nature can do and of the scale on which she operates is an intensification of the delusion that she has been conquered and outdone. When a man had accomplished some unusually impressive achievement it used to be said that he had "God's help." Nowadays we are more likely to assume that He needs ours.

But if nature, following her recognizable laws, made the Canyon "without human aid," then why did she do so many unusual things at this particular spot? Consider, to begin with, the most obvious anomaly. The mile-deep gash is cut through a high plateau seven to eight thousand feet above sea level and surrounded everywhere by lower-lying lands. To get to it one must climb up, no matter from what direction one approaches. Why did not the Colorado, like a normal river, flow around this obstruction as rivers nearly everywhere flow around even mere hillocks when they come to them?

Two hundred years ago anyone who had asked such a question would have been compelled to conclude that the river had just happened to come upon this strange channel through the plateau, though that answer would leave him with the equally puzzling question of how the channel came to be there. By the middle of the nineteenth century any reasonably instructed person would have known that rivers do not *find* channels but *make* them and that, improbable as it seems, the Colorado must have cut a gash a mile deep through the rock. But how did it get up there in the first place?

Now that the channel has been cut, the river flows normally—always from a higher level to a lower until it emerges

Water doesn't run uphill

from the Canyon and flows finally into the Gulf of California. Seemingly, it must once have run uphill—defying the laws of nature in order that it might someday flow normally again. An improbable story indeed! And why, even now, is it a paradox among rivers because it does not, at the Canyon, drain the country through which it flows? Most of the water which falls upon the surrounding region to the south runs downhill, away from the river, instead of draining into it.

Some two hundred miles northeast of Grand Canyon the San Juan River, one of the tributaries of the Colorado, cuts a canyon of its own. It is something more than twelve hundred feet deep instead of five thousand, and its length is only six miles. But it looks in many respects like a miniature version of its grandiose brother, and on any scale except that of Grand Canyon itself it is quite a spectacle. Geologists will tell you that the first of the surviving rock formations through which the river cut is slightly older than that at the rim of Grand Canyon, but to the lay eye the walls appear much the same and they have been eroded into terraces somewhat similar. Moreover, it is, in one respect, even more abnormal-looking. The river twists and turns in so extravagant and seemingly senseless a fashion (six miles to go one straight line mile) that it has earned the name "Goosenecks." Seven times it doubles back in such a way that it flows almost parallel with itself, and the stream runs now in one direction, now in the other, with only a narrow rock between two opposing currents.

GRAND CANYON

One does not need to be trained to ask geological questions to be struck by the fact that this is not the way rivers swift enough to cut deep channels are accustomed to run. Swift rivers run straight; sluggish ones meander. Looking at the course taken by the now swift San Juan, one is likely to be reminded of some slow-moving brook lazing its way across a nearly flat meadow and running so feebly that the slightest impediments turn it aside as it follows the path of least resistance here and there across the flat surface. If such a meadow brook cut deeply enough, it would make its own "gooseneck" canyon. But of course it doesn't and it couldn't. It is not swift enough to cut much, and if it were swift, it would flow over the almost invisible little obstructions which now turn it this way and that. In fact, it meanders so irresolutely that it may vary its channel from time to time, leveling the meadow still further. But it will never cut a deep channel.

Obviously the San Juan at the Goosenecks must have been sometime a meandering stream. As a matter of fact, the Goosenecks form what geologists call "an entrenched meander." But what, one wonders, can have happened to turn this feeble little current into a torrent large enough and swift enough to cut through hundreds of feet of solid rock and yet not make the straight channel to be expected of a swift river?

Probably, one will think first of the possibility that the earth, in one of her periodic convulsions, suddenly raised or tilted the flat surface across which the stream meandered,

Water doesn't run uphill

thus making it swifter and for some other reason more abundant. But that won't do. Tilt the meadow with its brook, and the stream will simply leap over the sinuosities of its low banks to take a shorter cut from high ground to low. Under those conditions it might cut a channel but it would not be the channel of its old meander.

There is, however, an obvious explanation of the anomaly. The land must have risen, but risen so slowly that the stream was never dumped out of its channel; so slowly, indeed, that it deepened this channel as fast or faster than the land rose and thus preserved the same course it had taken when it was too feeble to do more than obey the demands of every minor variation in level.

The explanation would never have been accepted by, and would probably never have occurred to anyone two centuries ago. Like all the explanations offered by geology today, it assumes vast stretches of time and assumes that the earth has existed for very much longer than anyone formerly dreamed that it had. The belief that its age was measured in a few thousands, not in many millions of years, was supported by the Biblical story. But even without that, the assumption was almost inevitable to a creature who instinctively measures things on a scale related to his own experience. It just didn't seem probable that anything had endured so much longer than man or the history he knew. Yet the existence of the Goosenecks and the Canyon—for which no credible explanation not involving millions of years is discoverable—is just one of the many kinds of things which

GRAND CANYON

gradually forced upon the human mind the intellectual conviction that the mountains, plains, and rivers among which man passes his brief life are old beyond his power to grasp, and make demands on his imagination that it can hardly compass.

Was Grand Canyon formed in precisely the same way as its small brother, the Goosenecks? Though many nineteenth-century geologists thought so, it is now generally believed that the explanation is not quite so simple. The Colorado also winds back and forth, but its meanderings are probably, in part at least, the result of rock structures encountered during its downward progress. It is not, in other words, merely the entrenchment of early meanders. But the essential fact that remains is this: The Colorado, like the San Juan, once flowed across flat country which lay at approximately the level of the present stream bed. It had climbed no mountains to get there; resisted no impulse to run steeply the shortest way downhill; and its height above sea level was not greater than it is now. The river, though it cut through rock now forming the rim, was never "up there."

Slowly, however, the earth began to rise under the river —never fast enough to dump it out of its channel, never so fast that it could not cut downward more rapidly than the earth rose. At the same time, the Colorado was becoming a mightier river. When the Rocky Mountains first rose, they had brought down more water and made or increased western rivers. Later, as each of the successive ice ages ended,

Water doesn't run uphill

melting snow and ice brought flooding waters and with them
the sand and pebbles and stones with which the river cuts
downward—not so much like the knife with which it is commonly compared, as like a file or a cutting disk well supplied
with abrasive. Moreover, as geologists are fond of pointing
out, the process was not like pushing a knife into a cake,
but like raising the cake slowly upward against an immobile
knife.

No one knows why the earth rises, falls, and sometimes
buckles or breaks in its alarming way. But it has done just
that many times in the past and is doing it now. A year or
two ago one of the Galápagos Islands rose with such unusual suddenness that what had been a bay became a shore.
The Himalayas are believed to be still in the making, and
Mount Everest is said to be rising. Parts of the California
coast are also rising; other parts of the United States sink-
ing. Whether or not the rocks of the Canyon walls and
floor are still moving upward, no one knows, though earth-
quakes in the region suggest that they may be, and there is
plenty of cutting power still left in the Colorado. In recent
times it has carried as much as 27,000,000 tons of sand and
silt past Bright Angel Point in one day and probably averages more than half a million—another reminder that "human aid" couldn't approximate its work.

Mountains are still a great deal more massive than skyscrapers. The most awesome force that man-induced atomic
fission has ever released is puny by comparison with that un-
leashed in a hurricane, to say nothing of that which lifted

GRAND CANYON

the Rockies and the Alps. If, as park naturalists often point out, the Empire State Building had been built on the river, its summit would be just barely visible from the rim as it peeped above the inner gorge some four thousand feet below. That the Colorado dug out what our bulldozers could not is even more vividly suggested by a comparison with the work done on the Panama Canal.

That, I suppose, represents man's greatest attempt to rival nature as an earth mover. It involved the stupendous task of moving something like 450,000,000 cubic yards of dirt and stone. But the Colorado moves about 170,000,000 cubic yards *per year*—or more than a Panama Canal-full every three years. And it has been working—at various rates, of course—for several millions of years!

3

Still in the making

When did all this happen? When did the land begin to rise and the river to cut downward? How long have at least the beginnings of the Canyon been there?

No one knows exactly. Estimates have varied all the way from one to several million years. But on any scale except the human the discrepancy is not very great, and today the one-million-year estimate is generally regarded as untenable. A million or seven million years is a short time as geology goes and not so very long ago. In any case, the Canyon is what has been described as "a youthful geomorphic feature." In general valleys and canyons are likely to be the youngest grand features of any landscape except those for which recent volcanic action is responsible.

Take even the discredited million-year estimate, and that would mean that the beginnings of the Canyon go back to about the time of the earliest half-man. Take the seven million, and it would already have been imposing by the time the first recognizable human existed anywhere. But in either case, the presence or absence of the nearly human would be the only really major difference so far as life on earth is concerned. Seven million years ago mammals were already becoming dominant, and flowering plants were already more successful than the fernlike and horsetail-like vegetation of earlier times. Seven million years ago there may have already been pony-sized horses on the American plains, though they were later to disappear and the horse was re-introduced by Europeans. A million years ago one of the great ice ages was about to begin and the woolly mammoth to flourish.

At whichever time the cutting may have begun, it was long after the last of the giant reptiles had perished and after his hardened footprints had already been buried beneath hundreds of feet of the shale and sandstone which had to be washed away before the footprints were again exposed. They can still be seen not many miles away. And as the river sawed slowly through the rising strata, its deepening walls exposed again to sight older and older formations going back more and more millions of years until, finally, they add up to more than a billion. Nowhere on the earth's sur-

Still in the making

face (except possibly on the Canadian Shield) are to be seen rocks older than those which form the sides of the Canyon's inner gorge.

What has all this to do with the beauty of the Canyon or with the peace and quiet and solitude to be found on its rim? Some would answer "nothing," and for them that answer is perhaps correct. But it is not the only one. Spaciousness has a great deal to do with the sense of peace and quiet and solitude, and spaciousness can be temporal as well as dimensional. Seated at any point on the rim, I look up and down as well as east and west, and the vista is one of the most extensive ever vouchsafed to man. But I am also at a point in time as well as in space. The one vista is as grandiose as the other. I am small and alone in the middle of these great distances, vertical as well as horizontal. But the gulf of time over which I am poised is inconceivably more vast and much more dizzying to peer into.

There is also another, less intangible reason why even as a spectacle the Canyon is absorbing almost in direct proportion to one's understanding of its structure. The fantastic —and at first sight it seems *merely* fantastic—is only momentarily arresting. Nothing that is without rhyme or reason can hold the attention for long. Hence the Canyon takes a firmer and firmer grip as the logic behind the seemingly illogical begins to reveal itself. Why, one begins to ask, these varying colors, these oddly sculptured pinnacles, these walls, slopes and terraces sometimes sloping steeply, sometimes ly-

GRAND CANYON

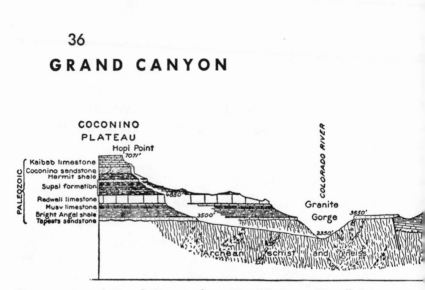

Cross section of Grand Canyon from Hopi Point to Tiyo Point.

ing almost flat in broad plateaus and sometimes dropping vertically down?

The first few hundred feet below the rim are nearly vertical; next comes a gentle slope broken by towers and turrets; then, after another vertical cliff, a broad, almost level plateau; and finally, the sheer drop into the inner gorge, at the bottom of which the river races and foams over rapids and shallows. The schematized outline is shown in the cross section.

And the most obvious questions are simply these: Why is it so much wider at the top than at the bottom? Why is there in some places an inner gorge into which the river fits snugly

Still in the making

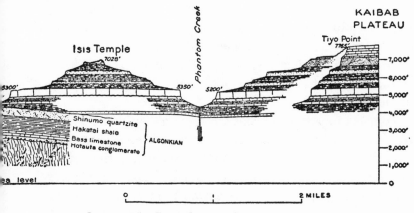

From the U.S. Geological Survey Map.

and which is not very much wider at the top than at the bottom? Surely the river was never ten miles wide and surely it has not gone on shrinking progressively as it cut deeper and deeper.

Of course not. All valleys widen as time goes on. In fact, that is why most rivers make valleys, not canyons. But if most rivers make valleys, then why did the Colorado make a canyon, and why has it obviously widened so much more at the top than toward the bottom?

To the first of these questions, "Why a canyon and not a valley?" the answer is that special conditions other than the slowly rising land existed here. River courses usually become valleys because, as the courses cut downward, water, frost, and the other forces of erosion break down the sides so rapidly that the valley becomes wide faster than it grows deep and, other things being equal, the less the cutting force of the stream, the wider the valley will be in proportion to its depth.

To make imposing canyons you need a considerable river carrying a large amount of abrasive material. But that river must flow through an arid country where the breaking down and widening of the sides will take place more slowly in proportion to the downward cut than it does in regions of normal rainfall. Because the rainfall in the West is so much less than in most other parts of the United States, the West is a country of canyons, great and small, as the East is a country of valleys. And because all the conditions for canyon-making were realized more extravagantly by the Colorado River and the region through which it ran than anywhere else on the globe, its canyon is the most triumphant example of what a river can do. There was the rising land; the swift, sand-filled river; and the arid country.

But why the deep, steep-sided V of the inner gorge in the Bright Angel area and the sudden opening out at its rim, so that the gorge makes almost a canyon within a canyon? Of course, the inner gorge was more recently cut, but not much more recently than the broad plateau which seems to separate it from the higher, wider portions might suggest. The answer, as we shall see when we get down there, is that the gorge is cut in a different, much harder, much more resistant rock. The plateau and all the successive strata above it are sedimentary rocks laid down as sand, mud and lime either underwater or on the surface of some ancient desert. But the rocks of the inner gorge are black, terribly hard, and so ancient that their earliest history is largely a matter of conjecture. Molten rock forced up through cracks from below has made great vertical seams of granite, but they are young by comparison with the older mass which goes back to that most ancient of all times, called the Archean. Undoubtedly, parts of it, too, were sediment in some past, a billion years ago, but it has been so heated and compressed and torn that its aboriginal character has been lost and it is very hard. The river must have cut very slowly through it, and weather has been able to affect very little its nearly vertical walls. Had all the rocks of the Canyon been equally hard, it might be now much less deep but much more narrow than it is.

Every cliff and terrace and pinnacle above the gorge is the result of differential weathering—the flats where some homogeneous stone has worn evenly away, the cliffs where something more resistant has stood boldly up, the pinnacles and mesas often the result of some cap of hard stone which has protected softer layers underneath, though they have been washed away everywhere else, thus leaving a pillar or a table still standing because protected from above. Or, if you prefer more technical language, a geologist will tell you that the plateaus are "geomorphically homogeneous" while "the stepped topography is due to the fortuitous alternation of beds having widely different resistance to erosion." He will add that drainage systems flowing down the sides have increased the variety with side canyons and amphitheaters; also that the varying colors which give to the exposed walls a sort of tuttifrutti appearance result from the equally fortuitous circumstance that there was "an alternation of light colored beds and dark colored beds, with the striking red beds in intermediate position."

When one has been talking in terms of millions of years, it is difficult to realize that the Canyon is not finished, that it is not made but in the making. Since the river still runs swift and still carries a tremendous load of cutting material, it must still be slowly wearing away the very hard Archean rock over which it runs—though unless the land is still rising (as it may be), it will cut more and more slowly as the gradient diminishes. On the other hand, the Canyon is getting wider much more rapidly than it is getting deeper, and the widening, unlike the deepening, is visually evident. Many of the large rock masses which form the promontories upon which visitors walk out for the best views into the depths are obviously separating from the rim by large cracks. The timid sometimes refuse for that reason to trust themselves to the rocks, though many will no doubt still be there hundreds of years hence. Other, smaller, boulders are more precariously attached, and looking over the rim one may see where still others broke loose, fell hundreds of feet

Still in the making

down, rolled a hundred more along some slope, and finally came temporarily to rest—temporarily because it is inevitable that the new support will someday be washed away from under them.

Even more striking are the still fresh scars on the sides of the vertical cliffs where great slabs, many tons of weight, have sloughed off, crashed into fragments where they struck, and then poured a stream of debris across terraces and down new cliffs. Inevitably, Bright Angel Lodge, if it stands long enough, will someday tumble into the chasm which now opens perhaps a hundred feet from its edge; the lodge on the north rim will fall even sooner, because it is closer to the disintegrating rim.

The cause of the widening, operative wherever any canyon or valley exists, is running or falling water, wind, the expanding roots of plants which get a foothold in crevasses and, where the weather is cold enough, the expansive force of freezing water which, like the roots, widens the cracks in which it gathers. The geologist, Edwin D. McKee, who has closely studied the process at Grand Canyon, thinks that the running and falling water is here very much the most important factor—especially the water which falls in the cloudbursts of summer and that which runs over the edge during the spring melting of the snow. At both such times sheets of water pour over the rim, remorselessly nibbling away limestone and sandstone, and shale, most of which were laid down under the same element that will reduce them ultimately to sand again.

GRAND CANYON

How fast is this happening? No one, so far as I know, has attempted to measure or even to estimate the rate at which the average distance between the two rims is increasing. But at least it is not so very slow as earth changes are measured. Major rockfalls, not to mention the minor ones, are relatively frequent. Some years ago, Emory Kolb, who had spent ten years on the rim, could report seven major falls within sight of his house, besides many others which could be heard. One, on the north rim just opposite Grand Canyon Village and plainly visible from there, was also audible across the ten airline miles between Village and opposite rim. During a thunderstorm in December, 1932, a great promontory just west of the Kolb studio dropped as a single mass and came to rest on the Supai formation more than a thousand feet below the rim. On a recent visit I noticed a huge fresh scar where a tremendous block which must have weighed many tons had broken off in 1954 from near the top of the Coconino sandstone (i.e., some five hundred feet below the rim). The major part of it lies now in fragments about three hundred feet lower, while a diminishing cascade of smaller and smaller fragments stream several hundred feet still farther down.

If the earth's crust in this region lies quiet for a time long enough, Grand Canyon will become a wide valley and finally, if time is still longer, a flat plain, all the successive layers of stone washed away, leaving the river to meander again as it once did—like an oversized brook across an oversized meadow.

Still in the making

Improbable? Already hundreds of feet of rock, laid down before the plateau was lifted to its present height, have disappeared completely, though they are still to be found on higher ground not far away. Time and time again in the earth's history "geomorphic features" more massive than the Grand Canyon have been leveled and obliterated only to have equally imposing features built again, either because the surface was forced up or because lava streams welled up from the earth's bowels.

As a matter of fact, this sort of thing has happened twice right where the Canyon now lies. To see the evidence of that we need to descend the mile below the rim and meet some of the oldest rocks face to face. But that journey had best be postponed for a while.

Meanwhile, a good way to dispel the human-aid delusion and the false sense of scale upon which it is founded is to probe the depth gingerly by strolling a mile and a half down the least used of the two principal trails which lead from the south rim to the bottom—remembering as you go that though you may stroll down to the bottom, you cannot stroll back up again. Such a mile and a half's probe will carry you only about eight hundred feet in vertical distance, but that is far enough to make the wall at one's back tower as high as all but the tallest skyscrapers, while the depths have not been brought detectably nearer. The broad Tonto Plateau, almost three thousand feet below the rim, looks just as far away as it ever did, and the bottom of the gorge is still usually invisible.

But though you seem to have made no progress toward plumbing the depths, you have already passed through quite a variety of changing scenes. For one thing, it is noticeably warmer, since to go eight hundred feet down is equivalent to going nearly five hundred miles southward, and the vegetation is noticeably different. So, too, are the color and the texture of the rocks and the shapes into which they have been sculptured. At first one zigzagged down two almost vertical walls, of grayish-white limestone separated by weak red sandstone. At about five hundred feet is sandstone of a slightly different color and so obviously different a texture that the line which marks the division between the two is clearly visible. This third layer is not quite so thick as the first two combined—something more than three hundred instead of something more than five hundred feet—and at just about the end of the mile-and-a-half walk it also suddenly ends where it rests upon a wall of red stone more startlingly different from either of the three previous walls than they are from one another.

The tops of the first mesas and buttes into which certain other rocks have been formed are mostly still below, and for some distance yet the steep wall down which one has been climbing is a wall and no more—sometimes almost perfectly vertical and everywhere cleanly rather than fantastically cut. Your walk will end near the top of this fourth layer, and on the exposed surface of a slab just by the side of the trail you will see very plainly impressed the neat double row of small footprints left by some four-footed creature when the rock was sand.

Any geologist will tell you that when you stood at the rim you were standing upon limestone laid down at the bottom of a shallow sea during the Permian period or, according to recently revised estimates, about 200,000,000 years ago; that your descent of some eight hundred feet had carried you back only a few million years farther without taking you beyond the limits of the Permian; and that these prints were made by some beast—perhaps reptilian, perhaps amphibian—who passed by there before the dinosaurs had got a start. They are real footprints in the sands of time; by comparison, the most enduring metaphorical one left by the most ambitious and most successful of men are written in water.

Suppose there had been no geologist conveniently at our elbow. What could a reasonably observant person see for himself, what sort of notions could he form of the meaning of what he saw; what tentative theories advance of the how and the why?

This is the sort of question I have frequently asked of myself when faced with some natural phenomena I could glibly explain on the basis of what other men had learned. And the answer I am compelled to give is usually sufficiently humiliating to myself. I would not know much about the world I live in had I been compelled to depend upon my own observations. The only consolation is that most men would have to admit that, and even the best men have seldom advanced knowledge more than a short step.

Nevertheless, we may, I think, pay ourselves the compliment of assuming that our short walk would have taught us something. The grandness of the scale, which is obvious as soon as you get into the Canyon instead of merely looking at it, would have disposed of the notion that man had had anything to do with the formation, and I like to think that the theory of a great crack in the cooling surface of a molten earth would also have been disposed of by the obvious fact that the rock wall is not homogeneous and that the different kinds of stone are obviously in layers, one on top of the other.

In most places on earth exposed rock strata are exposed only to a shallow depth and are also so tilted, broken or twisted that their character does not thrust itself upon the attention. But at Grand Canyon they have lain so quietly while they were sliced through like a layer cake that it seems almost as though they had been provided for the special purpose of demonstrating to an unobservant mankind that one great class of rocks are not the result of the cooling of a molten mass but that such rocks were, as the geologist says, "laid down," often one on top of the other. As the distinguished geologist, Charles Schuchert, once wrote on the Canyon, "Such a geological insight into the structure of the earth's outer shell is nowhere else to be had."

Just possibly I might have noticed for myself that em-

Still in the making

bedded in the topmost layer are fragments which upon close examination are obviously bits of sea shell and of coral, and if I had noticed that, I would probably have wondered, as men wondered for so many years after fossils had become quite well known, how the devil they got there. But I doubt very seriously that I would have noticed a difference between the texture of the upper two and the third layers which are otherwise so similar—a difference obvious enough when pointed out and consisting in the fact that whereas the topmost formations are composed of thin layers separated by almost perfectly horizontal lines, similar lines in the layer below run in sloping curves which seem to outline subsequently buried humps—so that it is, as the geologists say, "cross-bedded." And even if I had noticed that, I am pretty sure the explanation, again convincing enough once it has been suggested, would not have occurred to me. The top two layers are solidified lime which fell quietly to the bottom of quiet seas and lay there undisturbed; the next layer is of wind-blown sand, the outline of whose dunes, later covered by more sand, is so clear that from their outline —steeper on one side than on the other—one can see even from which direction the prevailing winds once blew over that desert.

Would I have done any better, or done even so well, with the question raised earlier, not how the rocks got there, but how they had been slashed through? Looking through binoculars at the opposite wall, ten miles away, I could hardly have missed the fact that rock layers in the two walls match.

GRAND CANYON

Each conspicuous layer corresponds to a similar layer on the opposite side. The conclusion that they continue one another, or rather that they would if the great gash had not been cut, is irresistible. Would I have assumed some violent catastrophe which cut or broke it in a relatively brief time? Or would the fact, evident enough in the great masses of rock cracked off from the sides and waiting to fall, or the other great masses lying where they have fallen, have suggested that since the whole face of the region is certainly still slowly changing, then the grand features themselves might have resulted from slow change? If I had indeed concluded something of the sort, then would I have gone on to suppose that the river, glimpsed from some point on the rim, had done the job?

Give me the benefit of a large doubt and suppose that I would have. The largest difficulty would still remain. I would still have been faced with the problem of getting the river "up there" where, as a matter of fact, it never had been. Would I have solved that problem, too? I very much doubt it. But it is some consolation to know that much simpler problems in geology did not suggest their obvious answers until a few generations ago, and that details concerning the Canyon are still being discussed as new facts come to light.

4

Journey in time

The Canyon has always had a great many European visitors. They are generally very appreciative, and rangers remark sadly that they are also much better informed, much better prepared to understand what they see, than the average American who frequently checks it off his list as he checks Notre Dame or St. Peter's in his guidebook. Sometimes, however, the European permits himself to remark that Grand Canyon, being American, is of course the *biggest* this, the *longest* that, and the *most* several other things in the world. And of course it really is.

GRAND CANYON

In some ways the most significant of its "mosts" is this: nowhere else on the surface of the earth is so long a stretch of geological time exposed in such undisturbed, easily read layers. The distance of one vertical mile traces the history of something like a billion years, and they can be covered without hardship in a few hours' time. All this history is, to be sure, very ancient history. One must start the journey in time a good many million years ago during the Permian period. But that is not, comparatively speaking, so very long ago, after all, and when one gets to the bottom one will be walking on rocks already formed at a time further removed from the first identifiable fossil structures than the time of those fossils is removed from our own day.

The best way to make this stupendous journey is on the back of a mule which makes it scores of times a year without becoming any the wiser in geology and without developing an interest in the scenery. But he has become very wise indeed in all that is required to negotiate safely and with a minimum of trouble to himself the seven miles of narrow, twisting trail necessary for the mile of vertical descent. Of course, you can walk if you prefer, but most—especially those who have sauntered down a mile or two and then struggled back—prefer the mule. Like the descent to Avernus, the descent of the Canyon is easy; but the coming up again is hard. Somehow the trail has become much steeper as well as much longer than when one went down, and walkers who have heard that the earth is sometimes thrust up are often inclined to believe that the trail was tilted while they were at the bottom.

One of the oldest white man's trails to the river—no longer used except occasionally by walkers—is called the Hance, after that John Hance at whose tumbling cabin the lizards now keep their court. This Hance, who made or at least began it for his own use and that of other early hunters, was a somewhat mysterious character who responded to all questions about his past by declaring that he "did not like ancient history" and is believed to have come to the Canyon from somewhere in Texas about 1880, though probably not by the method he liked to describe to tenderfeet—i.e., on the back of one of a herd of buffalo upon which he dropped from a tree. Later he acted as guide to those few early tourists—including Theodore Roosevelt—who came before the park was established. Later still he declined into a professional "character" employed by the Fred Harvey Company after 1903 to furnish atmosphere—which he generated abundantly by telling very tall tales. But he had been a real character before he took it up as a profession and he was among the first to clamber down from the rim. As Buckey O'Neill, another old-time figure, said: "God made the Canyon, John Hance the trails. Without the other, neither would be complete."

The general course of Bright Angel Trail, the most used by tourists, had been followed for no one knows how many years by the Havasupai Indians, who then farmed the watered area on the Tonto Plateau which lies more than 2,300 feet below the rim. About 1890 two miners reworked it and charged a toll to prospectors going back and forth to the mining claims which were later declared invalid. In 1928 it was acquired by the Park Service and since then it has been trod thousands of times by mules who seem to delight in terrifying their riders by facing meditatively outward toward the abysses it skirts before they turn daintily to face down the trail again.

Since this is to be a journey through climates as well as through time, it is just as well to choose carefully a good season of the year. The head of the trail, at seven thousand feet, is in a region where the sun is warm even in winter and the nights coolish even in summer. But the five-thousand-foot drop to the bottom is equivalent climatically to a journey of some three thousand miles southward. We start from an upper Sonoran zone where the dominant vegetation is the juniper and descend to a subtropical climate approximately equivalent to that of central coastal Mexico. Since that means intolerable heat in summer, we chose for this visit a day in early October. That means that even on the rim sunny days will be warm though the nights are chilly, while at the bottom—climatically three thousand miles farther south—the days will not be oppressively hot. At ten in the morning we mount our mules who appear to be perfectly aware of what is coming and mulishly resigned. But if one unneeded member of the string is left behind, he will bray dismally as his companions start off.

Journey in time

Before we take the first step downward we might as well consider what we start from. It is, of course, the high, dome-shaped plateau we climbed, no matter from which direction we approached the Canyon. Far to the north, higher cliffs are just visible, and to the southeast the 12,600-foot volcanic peaks of the San Francisco Mountains. Where we stand the soil is so thin that the underlying limestone is frequently visible, and the climate is too arid to support a very luxuriant vegetation. The dominant plants are juniper and the small piñon pine whose nuts were once so important to the Indians and are still so important to various forms of wildlife. The general effect on the flat is of some rocky seacoast, though the jays that sail into the trees, the ground squirrels which scamper at our feet, and the deer that peer at us from a safe distance, are sufficient reminder that this is mountain not coast.

The many shell fragments embedded in limestone under our feet are evidence enough that we are standing on what was once the bottom of some sea, and the paleontologists say that the creatures which secreted these shells belong to species which lived during the Permian, the last major division of the Paleozoic era—which means some 200,000,000 years ago. The geologists have named it the Kaibab limestone, and it once lay far below, down there below sea level. It was lifted to its present position a few million years before our time. Those higher cliffs dimly visible to the north represent sediments laid down many millions of years later than our Kaibab limestone and there the Kaibab is buried beneath thick layers of the younger rocks of which almost no trace is now to be found at the Canyon itself.

Was the Kaibab on which we are now standing once similarly buried? If so, then what has become of these later formations. Such questions we had better postpone. They do not concern us now. The distant cliffs are many years younger than any now visible at the Canyon, though they were formed long before the cutting began. We are starting with the present-day rim which was already nearly two million years old when the Canyon began to form. And all in all there is a lot of this particular formation. Exposed or buried, it grows thinner eastward and thus suggests that the warm shallow sea which laid it down came in from the west and northwest.

What was the world like and what was this particular region like at that geologically not very remote day when the first beginnings of the Canyon were visible to whatever creatures had by that time eyes good enough to see it with? Certainly, the Canyon was still young during the Pleistocene. That meant violent changes of temperature from cold to warm and back again as the ice to the north advanced and retreated, and with the changes in temperature went changes in plant and animal life. But most of it was already "modern," and could we see either the plants or animals, most would not strike us as outlandish or monstrous.

The dinosaurs had all disappeared long ago and the age of the mammals had long since dawned. Many plants now bore flowers; trees included the hardwoods and were not all the conifers and the overgrown ferns and horsetails they once had been. There were birds; there were bearlike animals; and there were horses. But there were no men or even sub-men anywhere in the world. Evidence is accumulating that the ancestors of the present-day Indians must have come across from Asia rather longer ago than used to be thought, but the length of their residence here is certainly measured in thousands, not hundreds of thousands, of years. No human being saw the Canyon until it was more or less what it is today, but keen mammalian eyes did see it in its youth, and the creatures, though strange, were not the nightmares of a still earlier time.

Suppose we ask now, not what the world was like when the Canyon first began to be a canyon, but at the far remoter time when the Kaibab limestone was being formed. The answer to that question raises before us a very different picture indeed, since the sea which laid it down had receded some 200,000,000 years before the limestone began to rise under the river which was to slice it through.

No record of anything that happened during the great stretch of time between the two events is to be found here. To find it we would have to go to the cliffs to the north, where we would find footprints of the dinosaur which dominated the earth for a far longer period than man has been in existence. But at Grand Canyon there is no trace of them because all the formations which record earth-history between the time when the sea retreated to leave the Kaibab dry and the present time had been eroded away before the Canyon was cut.

So far as the stone we are standing on is concerned, it takes us back at one great step across the age of mammals and all the great Mesozoic era of reptiles, back to the end of the Paleozoic when there were not only no mammals but no flowering plants and few if any land animals except insects, scorpions, spiderlike creatures, amphibia and small reptiles. On those parts of the earth which were land, scorpions crawled and dragonflylike insects flew. The land, which had long been without plant or animal life, was now green with the giant ancestors of horsetails, club mosses and seed ferns whose leaves and stems, after they died, were in some regions turning into coal. But there are no remains of any of these land dwellers in the Kaibab—only the shells, corals and sponges which lived in the obviously warm sea and the teeth of the sharks which swam through it.

This, then, is already very ancient history. Had we visited the region we would, to be sure, have recognized many of the plants and small animals as more or less like those among their descendants we are familiar with. But we would have missed everything we recognize as the "higher" plants and animals. We would have had the sense of being at the early dawn of our world. But ancient as the history of Kaibab is, we shall, as we descend into the Canyon, see nothing else so young. More and more time will drop behind us. And finally, before we reach the river, we shall be surrounded by an antiquity more remote than the mind can conceive.

The resigned mules need little urging. At the merest suggestion they plod forward, and though they will get only one rest some hours hence, they seldom require even a knee in their ribs—except from time to time when the fancy seizes them to nibble at some bit of half-green herbage beside the trail. But woe to the kindhearted rider who indulges his mount in this whim. He will find it stopping twice a minute if he has not been firm at the beginning. And long before he gets to journey's end he will regret not having proved at the start that he can be more stubborn than a mule.

In a moment we have dropped over the edge. And since the Kaibab cliff is one of the more precipitous, the voyager will soon have an opportunity to judge whether or not he is one of those to whom suspension over a precipice is no fun. The trail—just one mule wide—snakes back and forth along the face of the almost vertical wall into which it has been cut. Here at the very beginning as so often during the descent, there are only inches between the rider and a sheer drop of hundreds of feet. But the nonchalance of the mule —whose own neck is at stake—should reassure the riders. Obviously he is sure of himself even when he stumbles. He is bored rather than apprehensive. And when he comes to one of the cutbacks where another step forward would send him hurtling, he stops with his head over the edge of noth-

ingness, pivots slowly on all four legs, and slouches with
dragging hoofs down the reverse incline. Geology does not
interest him, though botany does. He is primarily interested
only in getting himself to the bottom and he will take care
of you incidentally while taking care of himself.

Throughout the first five hundred feet of vertical descent
even the observant will see little variation in the appearance
of the stone into which the trail has been hacked. It is all a
neutral limey gray, though the bottommost part (called
Toroweap) is believed to have been laid down by a sea
which advanced and then retreated before it came back
again to lay down the Kaibab. The two seas were similar and
not separated by any great interval as geological time goes.
The two strata are hardly distinguishable to the casual eye.
They are of similar color and texture and they are similarly
laminated into horizontal sheets but are separated by horizontal strata of red mudstone formed between invasions of
the sea.

For another three hundred feet below the five hundred
we have already descended the wall continues nearly vertical, but one does not need to be especially observant to note
that the stone is no longer the same. It is slightly more yellowish in color, different in texture, and no longer horizontally laminated. Instead of the horizontal lines of cleavage,
curved lines, one above the other, trace the outline of humps
steeper on the one side than the other. Clearly—once the
fact has been pointed out—sand dunes were successively
buried in more and more sand.

Journey in time

This is the Coconino sandstone which was once the surface upon which the first of the two intruding seas laid down the limestone, mostly shells and skeletons of marine animals. These dunes also belonged to the Permian, but the Permian lasted for perhaps thirty million years and within it there was lots of time for changes in climate and changes in levels. Like the Kaibab, the Coconino covers a lot of ground, something like thirty thousand square miles. The slope of the dunes suggests that the prevailing winds were from the north and that, from a desert lying in that direction, the sands were blown in. There is evidence also that in the region where they were being piled into dunes the climate was growing more and more arid so that it was at times almost a Sahara. Probably no considerable interval of time intervened between desert and sea bottom.

As one might expect, relics of animal life are not so abundant as in the Kaibab limestone. Seas teem, deserts do not. Besides, sea shells are much more readily preserved than bones. No actual vertebrate remains have so far been found in the Coconino. But it was certainly not a lifeless desert. Footprints of some small animals plodding always *up* a dune have been found, and the geologist, Edwin McKee, has produced prints almost precisely identical by chivying lizards up a dry sandy slope. Moreover, he has shown how the tracks might have been preserved if made in sand moist with dew and then covered with dry, wind-borne grains; also why the footprints always point upward: when a lizard crawls down a dune, sliding sand promptly fills his footprints. During no part of the Permian were there any land animals except salamanders, lizards and invertebrates, though insects were certainly in the air and millepedes and scorpions on the ground.

If Kaibab limestone means "sea" and Coconino sandstone means "desert," any kind of the rock called "shale" always means "mud." And the most unobservant traveler will observe that the yellowish or grayish cliff he has been descending for some eight hundred vertical feet rests squarely upon a thick layer of dark, rather slick-looking rock, even if he does not know that this smooth red rock is a shale.

By now the contour of the surface is changing also. The more or less uniform cliffs are giving way to the red buttes he admired from the rim, and between them the trail now threads its way. Heretofore, he has usually been able to see towering above him the rim from which he started; now it tends to disappear behind the buttes, and during the rest of the way to the bottom he will be able to glimpse it only from time to time. Far below lies a broad plateau which ends at another precipice plunging to the river below. But the river also is not usually visible from the trail. We are now lost in a wilderness of stone hills and mesas which provide no ultimate point of reference to guide us as we blindly follow the trail. Moreover, the air has begun to grow distinctly warmer, and the sparse vegetation has changed its character.

There are some eleven hundred vertical feet of this red shale, and though geologists divide it into the Hermit and the Supai, they are not so very different to the casual eye.

Journey in time

Both, like the Coconino and the Kaibab, belong still to the Permian period and both are composed of hardened sand and mud. Obviously, this region was neither a desert nor a sea when the shale was being formed. And the most evident proof is supplied by the rather abundant impressions of plant leaves and stems clearly and beautifully preserved in this mud-become-stone.

A number of especially handsome specimens of plant impressions are on exhibit in the museum on the rim. Most of them are fernlike and to the casual eye rather modern-looking, though most are probably not the immediate ancestors of our ferns but those seed ferns (so called because they bore true seeds rather than spores) which, for some odd reason, were much more common during this and somewhat earlier ages than true ferns were. There are still no true animal remains, but there are clear traces of animal life nonetheless—among others a beautifully clear impression of an insect wing four inches long and quite evidently from what we would have no difficulty in recognizing as a dragonfly. Such insects were among the earliest to inherit the earth, and from similar shale in other parts of the world it is known that some were monsters with a wingspread of nearly thirty inches—much greater than that of any of their dwindled descendants.

Amphibia and possibly reptiles were also common and they left abundant traces. In fact, the first evidence of vertebrate life ever found in the Canyon walls was the footprint of such an amphibian or reptile discovered in 1915 by the eminent geologist, Charles Schuchert. Since then many have turned up and several are exposed *in situ* along the trail for the benefit of travelers curious enough to wonder at these footprints in the muds of time.

All these creatures were small, weak and humble but they were on the way up. They were to go on increasing in strength and size for fifty or a hundred million years until, as dinosaurs, they became the largest land animals ever to shake the earth beneath their feet. Some pretty big ones were to leave footprints in other shale still surviving within a hundred miles of the Canyon. Later only smaller and smaller types survived, until today, instead of ruling the earth, the reptiles have every man's hand (and many a tooth and claw and beak) against them and manage to survive only by hiding under rocks and in swamps where few bother to seek them out.

Paleobotanists say that all of the plants in the shale were terrestrial. They include long extinct relatives of our club mosses (Sphenophylla, if you like long names) and early ancestors of our conifers—though, of course, none of the true flowering plants which were still millions of years in the future. Some of these plants were characteristic of rather arid regions and when you add to that two facts: first that certain moisture-loving plants of this same period are conspicuously missing and, second, that much of the sandy, mud-born shale fills arroyolike channels previously worn in an earlier rock, the picture seems clear. This region, which was later to become a sandy waste at the time of the Coco-

nino and still later to be covered by a shallow sea, was then
a rather arid flood plain traversed by streams coming from
the north.

All these processes which change landscapes and shift climates, which raise mountains only to wear them down
again, or spread deposits on top of older deposits, are going
on today as they had been going on for a time much longer
before the Hermit shale was deposited than has elapsed
since then. We would need a movie very much speeded up
indeed to be very dramatically aware of them, but they are
evident enough even now to those who look carefully.

Go, for instance, to the mouth of the Colorado where, a
few hundred miles from where we now stand, it empties
into the Gulf of California. There a delta plain some fifty by
twenty-five miles in extent is being slowly (in fact, rather
rapidly as such things go) built up out of the sand and silt
the river has carried away, some from the bottom of the
Canyon, more from the country to the north from whence it
and its tributaries flow. Not so very far north of that delta
but well west of the river the Salton Sea is rapidly (and to
the distress of farmers) increasing in size, though no one is
quite sure why. It lies nearly 250 feet below sea level and it
is possible at least that the water now held back by the delta
is seeping into it underground. If so, the whole rich Imperial
Valley may at some not very distant day be flooded with salt
water. But whether or not that ever happens, the delta is
shale in the making. Fragments of plant and animal life are
at this moment rotting away in the layers now covered

with fresh silt. Given time enough and the proper conditions, it will become something very much like the Hermit shale and subject, as the Hermit shale has been, to no one knows what future history. Someday geologists and paleontologists may be examining there a layer again exposed and deducing its age from what they find. But for our geological period they will have to find a new name. Nowadays it is called rather vaguely "recent." It will not be recent then.

What the geologist has to tell about the history of the Grand Canyon or about any other region of the earth we inhabit sounds like a very tall tale when we hear it first. Any healthily skeptical person who is asked to accept the conclusion without, like most persons, having ever thought much about the subject is excusable, even laudable, if he shrugs his shoulders and asks: "How can anyone know?" But though the subject is enormously complicated and the accumulated data confusingly multiplex, the methods and the *kind* of evidence dealt with are both quite easy to grasp, and the logic, as opposed to the confusing details of evidence, readily understandable. In fact, of all the modern sciences, the general procedures of geology are the most readily comprehensible to the layman.

In an earlier day science, in general, was sometimes called merely "applied common sense." To a great deal of it that description is no longer applicable. The biochemist, for example, cannot very well explain what he is doing to anyone who has had no preliminary training in the simpler aspects of his subject. The case of the new physicist is, of course, much worse. He announces conclusions and he demonstrates their validity by setting off an atom bomb. But not one man in a thousand can begin to understand either the instruments he uses, the evidence he collects, or the mathematics he calls upon to interpret it. Here is something so far from being applied common sense that even the physicist himself admits that it is, if not exactly nonsense, quite irreconcilable with everyday sense.

Geology, on the other hand, is still applied common sense, and the sense of it can be comprehended by any reasonably intelligent person who will listen. Indeed, he is likely, just because it is all so plain, to become overconfident. He will make rash deductions of his own on the basis of too little evidence. It is actually all too complex for any except the expert. But at least it is not esoteric. Moreover, it happens also that the story at the Canyon is unusually clear and uncomplicated. During relatively recent time, especially since the beginning of the Permian some 200,000,000 years ago, the history has been unusually continuous, disturbed by no phenomena more violent than the slow lifting of the sedimentary layers to the height they now occupy and without even much breaking or folding to confuse the record. A pedagogue could hardly have arranged a simpler, more diagrammatic demonstration. Indeed, geology here looks clearer and simpler than it usually is. A better first lesson could hardly be imagined than that we read on muleback descending from Kaibab, to Toroweap, Coconino, and then to the Hermit and Supai shale.

The somewhat sloping and much sculptured red shale ends as suddenly as the limestone and sandstone above it, and they end at the brink of another imposing cliff—the great Redwall as it is popularly called. From the rim no feature is more inevitably noticed than this brilliantly colored band which runs at almost the same height all along the Canyon's two walls, the north as well as the south. On our trail it averages some 550 feet thick, never departing far from the perpendicular but often leaning forward to make an overhang. We must snake our way back and forth across the face of this precipice, much as we did at the beginning of our journey, and as soon as we have begun to do so, we have left the Permian age, though not yet the Paleozoic era of which it is a subdivision.

Chip a piece of the Redwall and you will see that it is not red at all, except at the surface which has been stained by the iron oxide leached down from above. It is, instead, a blueish-gray limestone, very fine, uniform, and abounding in sea shells as well as in the remains of other forms of ocean life. It belongs to the period the geologists call the Mississippian, during which great coal deposits were made in warm swampy areas in some parts of the world, though there are no such beds here.

The Redwall is the creation of a sea far more imposing

than that which laid down the Kaibab. Its work can be traced many hundreds of miles to the north since this Mississippian ocean extended all the way from northern Canada down the western part of the continent to here. And for how long a time the region—later to be a desert and now after another watery interval to be semidesert again—was to remain beneath the sea! Long enough for 550 feet of limestone, mostly the hardened ooze of dead marine animals, to be built up, precisely as, at the bottoms of many of today's great oceans, the ooze grows deeper as a remorseless rain of little skeletons, the majority of them microscopic, come to rest at the bottom. The great Redwall is, in other words, a stupendous graveyard.

When we come at last to its base, we are upon the first flat surface since we left the rim—on a great plateau called the Tonto Platform. By now we have descended some 3,200 vertical feet from our starting point or just about halfway to the river. From the Bright Angel Lodge the Tonto seems to be the bottom, or does, at least, until one notices that it ends at another abyss into which one gets no glimpse, though one has been told that at its bottom the river, responsible for the whole of the Canyon, flows onward, cutting slowly still deeper.

This plateau—so different from any other feature of the Canyon—is a fascinating area. Seen from the rim half a mile higher it looks a vague gray-green, rather like what astronomers describe as the color of the supposedly vegetative areas on the planet Mars. And it does indeed have a flora and fauna of its own—both of which are typically Lower Sonoran, as contrasted with the Upper Sonoran of the south rim and the Transitional and Canadian of the higher north rim. Here at the proper season are birds not commonly found above: the desert sparrow, the lazuli bunting and the long-tailed chat. The dominant vegetation is the scraggly poor relation of the rose family sometimes called burrobrush, yucca, and the leafless green-stemmed ephedra or Mormon tea, concerning which last two things are notable: the first is that, like its Chinese relative which is exploited commercially, it contains the drug ephedrine used in the treatment of colds and asthma and thus demonstrates that it was not mere superstition that made the Mormons brew a medicinal drink from it. The second, more pertinent here, is that this ephedra is a primitive green plant whose early history is obscure but may be little changed since Paleozoic days.

After a wet spring the sago or Mariposa lily blooms here as it does in other Lower Sonoran deserts and so does the little purplish flowered filaree so common on cattle ranges, though it is not American at all, was probably unintentionally introduced in hay imported by early settlers, and has, nobody knows when, managed to colonize even this isolated plateau. Now in mid-October, 1956, after a summer even drier than usual, the plateau looks as deserty as any area not completely devoid of even the remains of vegetation can look. Even the burrobrush seems dry and dead beyond possible revival (though it is not), and one wonders what nourishment it can possibly give to the mules who will munch it solemnly if given a chance. Moreover, though we see none today, the Tonto is also the favorite haunt of those wild burros descended from work animals turned loose by despairing prospectors when, in the early days, they abandoned their claims. Park rangers do not regard them with much favor, because they eat the scant forage available to native animals.

On this platform, not far from the base of the Redwall is a clump of cottonwoods, the largest trees we have seen since we left the rim, and they are watered by the stream from a large spring. Nowadays much of the water from this spring is pumped the 3,200 vertical feet up to where it supplies all the needs of those who visit or live on the waterless rim. Long ago it irrigated the crops of the Indians living there, and now, realistically rather than fancifully, the small area still shaded by cottonwoods is called Indian Gardens. It is here that one usually stops to eat a picnic lunch and to stretch briefly one's stiffened legs. Later, if we like, we can go out across the plateau to the point where it drops off into the inner gorge and from which one can see the river another fifteen hundred feet below. But there is no descending there, and most travelers, realizing what is still ahead of them, elect no side trips. The practicable route is down a secondary canyon cut by the spring-fed stream which begins its descent near the Gardens themselves.

5

Farther journey in more time

Our journey in time from the Coconino rim to the Tonto Plateau was not smoothly continuous. We descended a slope which led downward and backward, seemingly step by step. Sometimes the physical incline was steep and sometimes gentle. Sometimes, also, we dropped without knowing it through a vacant abyss of time.

For instance: the Mississippian sea must have receded before the Supai shale was laid down upon it. The fact that here and there this shale fills deep gullies washed into the upper surface of the Mississippian is proof enough that

Farther journey in more time

there was a dry period during which the surface was exposed and eroded instead of built up. As the geologists would say, the shale rests "unconformably" upon the Mississippian sandstone—by which they mean simply that the more recent layer does not rest directly upon the original surface of the older. And as we continue our journey from rim to river, there are stupendous unconformities, abysses of time through which we must fall. Unknowingly we had dropped through one of them when we first found ourselves on the Tonto Plateau.

Coming down the trail we noticed nothing between the limestone of the Redwall and the hard rock of the plateau. But without knowing it we had stepped back through something like 200,000,000 years—which happen, moreover, to include three great geological ages which saw some of the most important of all the advances made during the long evolution of living things. We trod no record of the Devonian nor of the Silurian and the Ordovician during which occurred what was perhaps the greatest event since life arose: namely, the development of the first plants and the first animals to escape from the water to which all their ancestors had been confined and to begin the colonization of the land.

In the Hermit and Supai shale we had seen the tracks of amphibia or reptiles, the wing of a flying insect, and the fronds of fernlike plants. They could not have been there but for their adventurous predecessors—probably plants first of all and scorpions next—who had risked the great adventure of life in air rather than in water. Yet along our trail the record of these great adventures has been completely expunged. The surface on which we rested and lunched is composed of hard rocks originally deposited under a far earlier sea, and in places it is rich with the fossils of very primitive sea animals, all of which belong to the Cambrian or first age of the Paleozoic era and hence represent the earliest easily recognizable fossils anywhere preserved. But there is no record in Grand Canyon of the stages which were passed as these very early creatures evolved into the amphibia and reptiles who left their tracks in the Hermit and Supai shale. Obviously, then, though so much of the earth's early history can be read at Grand Canyon, not all of it is preserved there. Some very important chapters have been lost.

How do we know that the chapters are missing? First of all, just because there are no traces of the plants and animals which elsewhere record how life was developing during those years. Equally conclusive is the fact that in other parts of the Canyon wall (which our trail did not cross) some relatively thin layers dating from one of the otherwise missing ages are present. On our return journey up a different trail lying somewhat to the east we shall pass through what is left of the Devonian rocks and in such rocks remains of the expected very primitive fishes have been found. Everywhere in the Canyon, however, the Silurian and the Ordovician are completely missing, and the

Farther journey in more time

Redwall rests upon either a vestige of the Devonian or upon the Cambrian.

Such unconformities are frequent in the earth's crust. In fact, the section exposed at the Canyon is remarkable rather for its continuity than for the number of unconformities. And wherever—here or elsewhere—unconformities exist, they exist for one of two clear reasons.

Sometimes the missing strata never existed at that particular place. Between the time when one layer was formed and the next laid unconformably upon it, no building up took place. The area was neither sunk below the sea, flooded by rivers, nor piled high with desert sands. Instead, it rested quietly as the forces of erosion wore it down. In other regions certain strata were laid down but later rose and remained so long in an exposed position that they were entirely eroded away before conditions changed and new deposits were made. This obviously is what happened during Devonian times at the Canyon. Between that age and the age of the Mississippian Redwall so great an interval of wearing away intervened that in most places no trace remains of the deposits laid down during the intervening millennia, though elsewhere in the Canyon a little is still to be found.

The Cambrian lasted a long, long time, and as we follow the creek canyon downward we shall have time to become quite familiar with it. But before we start again, it will be worth while to stroll a few hundred yards east of our picnic place to look among the broken shreds of shale for one of the fossils which are quite abundant there. If we find one, it will probably be a trilobite, which is perhaps the commonest of the well-preserved fossils of very early age, and thousands have been collected at many different parts of the world.

Trilobites flourished for perhaps 200,000,000 years. They were the dominant animal during a considerable part of that era, and no other animal has ever been for so long a time the kingpin of creation. For these and for many other reasons a trilobite is worth looking at—especially if you can hold in your hand a four- or five-hundred-million-year-old specimen picked up on the very spot where it gave up its primitive ghost all those unimaginable millions of years ago. Trilobites were humble creatures but they were quite elaborately organized for all that and they were much the best that nature had been able to do after no one knows how many billions of years of trying. And though, shortly after the Kaibab limestone was being formed the race of trilobites disappeared so utterly that they have no very close living relatives, they lasted far longer than the dinosaurs were to last—to say nothing of man who, so far, has only a very brief history and may, for all we know, have only a very brief future. Trilobites had much better reason to suppose that the earth belonged to them than we have to assume that it belongs to us or that it was created primarily *for* us. If trilobites could have thought at all, they would probably have wondered, as foolish men still sometimes do,

Farther journey in more time

just which of their special needs this or that other living creature had been created to supply.

Though all were constructed according to the same general pattern, that pattern was such a good one for its time that a great many different species developed and they varied enormously in size. Some were no bigger than pinheads and some reached a length of two feet, though the largest found at the Canyon is only a little over three inches long.

Look at one of the fossils exhibited at the museum on the south rim. If you are very summary about such matters, you will probably say that it looks like some kind of bug; if you are more precise, that it suggests some sort of crustacean. And in the latter case you will be essentially right, though it is a very primitive sort of crustacean, and it was along about this time that the crustacea were separating from the arachnids or precursors of present-day mites and harvestmen. The name trilobite was bestowed because of the three lobes into which the body is divided, and the position in which some fossils have been found shows that some trilobites dating from the Ordovician or later could roll themselves into a ball like the pill bugs which infest damp spots in modern gardens.

Primitive though they are—and after all they are among the very first creatures with a sufficiently substantial outer shell (internal skeletons hadn't been invented yet) to leave fossils behind—they obviously represent a long development which had carried them hundreds of millions of years, perhaps a billion, away from the first just living organisms—

whatever they may have been like. They have eyes—many-faceted eyes like those of the housefly—and an eye is structurally an astonishing invention just as the ability to *see*, even when an eye has been provided, is something which defies the imagination. Probably they spent most of their time crawling over the ooze which was later to become Paleozoic limestone and by which they were covered when they died—just, we are likely to imagine, in order that we might come upon them in our turn. Some, at least, ate simple, unarmored contemporary creatures, and the trilobite must have been the terror of his age, the real king of the beasts in that day.

After a reign of some millions of years, trilobites suddenly disappeared at the end of the Permian—or about the time when the last of the Kaibab limestone (in which, as a matter of fact, trilobite fossils have been found) was being laid down. Thus the time that has passed since the last trilobite died is less than that which extended from the beginning of their domination to their extinction. But there is no trace of them during the 200,000,000 years since the end of the Permian. Why should a creature which lasted so long, which gave so magnificent a demonstration of fitness to survive, have become so suddenly (as such things go), utterly extinct?

It is easy to say that conditions changed and that trilobites could not adapt to them. But what conditions? That, it is impossible to say. Alternately, you may want to assume

Farther journey in more time

that bolder, stronger, more aggressive creatures destroyed the whole race. Yet the fact remains that other primitive animals which never flourished so exuberantly as the trilobites did have lasted down to the present almost unchanged and they seem to be getting along very well.

Sea scorpions came out of the water to become land scorpions something like a hundred million years later than the first trilobites swarmed in the same sea. They were not obviously better equipped for the struggle for life than trilobites were. Moreover, they have changed or adapted very little, while far stronger, more intelligent creatures have been disputing the earth with them. A present-day scorpion is very little different from his Silurian ancestors who walked along the shore while trilobites still swam in the oceans. Scorpions have already lasted something like a hundred million years longer than the trilobites did. And there is nothing to indicate that they may not be here a hundred million years longer.

"Dead as a dodo," we are accustomed to say. But the dodo has been dead only a couple of centuries and he had not lasted very long. "Dead as a dinosaur" would be better, because the last of these not-too-much-regretted monsters presumably died sixty or seventy million years before the last dodo was clubbed on the head. And man had nothing to do with the dinosaur's demise. But "dead as a trilobite" would be still better. Here is something that has been very dead for a really long time. Though he was the best that nature had been able to do up to that time, nothing deader can be imagined. He had his day—and a long one it was—but now he is only a fossil in a very ancient rock.

Is it possible that in some not thoroughly explored sea some trilobite, or at least some near relative, still prolongs in obscurity the life of his once royal race? Barely possible, perhaps, but extremely unlikely. One hesitates to say positively no, because representatives of supposedly extinct genera and even orders of both the animal and plant kingdoms do turn up unexpectedly from time to time. But the trilobite has been missing much longer. He should at least be listed among the very confidently presumed dead.

Why all this about a creature whose remains can be found a few hundred feet from our picnic spot but admittedly was neither very imposing nor very intelligent except by comparison with the even less advanced animals who, to their sorrow, had to share the Cambrian seas with him? There is one reason not yet alluded to. Of the two still living animals whose structure somewhat resembles his and which are believed by some to be his closest, though collateral, relatives, one is (*mirabile dictu*) to be found occasionally in temporary spring pools a few hundred yards from the Canyon rim. But that is another story.

The trail we now resume follows down the creek bed and thus off the plateau leading us through the whole thickness of the Cambrian rock in which are found both the earliest trilobites and, for that matter, the earliest (with one excep-

Farther journey in more time

tion) distinct traces of any kind of animal life. Before the
trail reaches the river it will traverse strata which are no
longer Paleozoic but belong to what has been called the
Protozoic era because, so it was presumed, there must have
been living then the naked, mostly microscopic, animals
which, like the present-day amoeba, are too insubstantial
to leave any trace.

But we do not move continuously from the Cambrian, or
earliest period of the Paleozoic, directly upon rocks of the
late Protozoic. Here we come instead upon another great
unconformity, representing an elapse of time probably
longer than that which separates the Cambrian from the
present day.

Even the traveler most completely innocent of any notions
of geology will notice that he is in a different world. The broken rocks over which his mule is now picking its way are
darker, grimmer, and, even to the most casual eye, suggest
a greater antiquity. It is difficult to imagine that they were
once (as they actually were) sedimentary deposits. Now
they are more crystalline than any we have seen before and
badly shattered. Moreover, the steep angle at which the
strata are tilted makes a striking contrast with the horizontal
layers of those above, which had so obviously lain quietly
ever since they were formed—even during the slow lifting
of the series as a whole while the river was slicing through
them.

Such tilted strata always mean that where they are found
the earth has endured one of the great heaving spasms

which make mountains. At some time long after they had been laid down, these Algonkian rocks, as the geologists call this Proterozoic formation, were heaved and broken into mountain ranges like those which still stand boldly up in the enormously younger Rockies. Moreover, so the geologists say, the structure or texture of the rocks is of a kind which results only from enormous pressures when the weight of a whole mountain rests upon them. Therefore, what we have left here are only the roots of once towering peaks which were slowly leveled during a time as long, perhaps, as it will take for erosion to reduce the Rockies themselves to their bases. Only after the high mountains had been leveled did the Cambrian sea flow in to teem with trilobites and other still humbler creatures which had come into existence between the time when the original mountains were lifted and the time at which they had already been worn down to those bases which still remain because they are now protected by all the layers above them. And it was on the surface of these bases that the Cambrian ooze settled down to make the surface upon which we ate our lunch.

By now we are only a few hundred feet above the river. There are no remains of the Algonkian rocks at this particular point, and we have not much farther to go before we reach the very bottom. But first we must drop through another inconceivable abyss of time.

Again even the least curious traveler will notice that he has entered into still another different world. This is the gloomiest, most forbidding part of the Canyon. The broken rocks are dark, almost black. Instead of the horizontal stratification which persisted through the younger limestone, sandstone and shale; instead of the abruptly tilted stratification of the Algonkian, we have here no detectable bedding of any kind. These rocks are only a crystalline mass, tremendously hard, brittle, and sparkling with mica. Through them run great vertical seams filled with dull rose quartz to complete a picture of utter confusion, and they tell to even the most expert geologist only a very summary story. They are vastly more ancient than the remains of the Algonkian rocks and they have had to endure even more. Except for the quartz seams, they, too, were presumably once sediments of mud or ooze or sand. But they have been so transformed by heat and pressure and time that there is little or nothing else about their origins to be read in them. They belong to the time which geologists call Archean or, sometimes, Azoic, because it may even be that they were first formed in some pre-prehistoric ocean or river or flood plain, before even the first blob of just living protoplasm had, somehow, appeared on earth.

But like the Algonkian rocks, they, too, represent the roots of once towering mountains which had been lifted and worn down almost to a plain again before the quartz was forced up molten from below into cracks; before the Algonkian sediments were laid down upon them; and, of course, before these last were tilted into high mountains only to be worn down again in their turn.

Algonkian rests unconformably upon Archean, and the

line between them is everywhere perfectly sharp and distinct. But it represents the elapse of a period of time at which the mind balks. You may span the physical record of the interval with the thickness of your finger. But you cannot span it with your imagination. How long in years shall we call it? Something like, say the geologists, 500,-000,000.

These Archean rocks are among the oldest exposed anywhere on the surface of the earth, though others of comparable age are in many high young mountains into which they were lifted in more recent upheavals and where they have been exposed by the weathering away of more recent layers. Deeper than these old rocks, the Colorado has not yet cut and perhaps never will, though below them must lie, in depths from which the once molten quartz was forced upward, the still hot materials that have never reached a cooling surface.

By now most travelers are glad that there are no farther depths into which they will have to make their way. For four or five hours they have been upon their steep winding descent. During a good part of that time they have been resting their weight upon a hand pressed against the pommel of their saddle to prevent themselves from going over the head of their mule and they are glad that the river has stopped where it has. Only glimpses of that river have been seen from time to time, but it is now in constant view as one follows for a mile or two eastward an almost horizontal

Farther journey in more time

trail blasted in the face of the Archean cliff to the one-mule-wide suspension bridge which will carry them across the river to their lodging for the night or—if they are wise—for two or three.

This bridge, completed in 1928, is 420 feet along its roadway and sixty above normal water level. It is the only possible crossing in the more than two hundred miles between Navajo Bridge to the east where the Canyon is narrow and just beginning, and Lake Mead to the west. One looks down at the river with a new respect. Can it really have done all the work one has seen in a matter of a few million years? The fact that it now carries an average of nearly a million tons of abrasive sand and silt past this point every day makes it easier to understand. Still one can forgive the remark of the disgruntled visitor to the rim who exclaimed: "Just my luck to come to the Canyon at a time of year when there isn't any water in it."

Once across the bridge it is only a matter of about half a mile more to Phantom Ranch, a collection of substantial little cabins and a dining hall. This must certainly be one of the most inaccessible places of public resort in the world. Suppose the little bridge were swept away, then the only practical escape would be up the fourteen-mile-long trail to the north rim, more than a mile above our heads and, arrived there, one would be some hundred miles from a railroad.

Yet though Phantom Ranch is very simple, there is nothing particularly austere about it. The cottages are comfortable, the food good. Bright Angel Creek, which rises not far beyond the north rim and comes down through a side canyon of its own, gathering in its course tributaries from springs in the walls, supplies an abundance of clear cold water. Some hours before we set out from the opposite rim, a pack train loaded with food and general supplies—including feed for the mules—had set out and had arrived before us. We will eat a hearty ranch-style dinner and stretch our aching limbs on a comfortable bed.

The entire journey down has been through scenes indescribably grandiose, often between colorful hillocks and buttes but always austere and sometimes, especially within the inner gorge, somber almost to the point of gloominess. Vegetation was sparse and obviously just surviving; animal life extremely scanty. One was constantly reminded of terrific forces, vast stretches of time, and the death of whole races of once flourishing living creatures now reduced to a few mineralized skeletons or a few impressions in the hardened mud, and it is easy to realize how desolate and terrifying it all was to those earlier explorers who were completely alone in a forbidding, seemingly accursed land where nature was many things but certainly not kindly.

Here now at the bottom she smiles again. Water brings life, and wherever there is life, there is beauty and a sense of joy. Bright Angel Creek makes a kind of oasis. Birds again inhabit the trees; along the stream bank for miles scarlet monkey flowers and Cardinal flowers draw, even in mid-October, a curving red line. That sense of being al-

Farther journey in more time

most perilously cut off from the rest of the world which one ought perhaps to feel is reduced to no more than an agreeable feeling of peaceful retirement. The little oasis one has come to rest in is snug and cozy, and though surrounded by buttes and cliffs, they so cut off the view in most places that had one been taken here blindfolded one would never guess how deep he was below all the surrounding country except the channel of the river.

If, however, the long journey down has soon begun to seem unreal, and if one would like to recover it, that is easy, too. The corral where we dismounted is one of the few places from which the rim can be seen, and seen, actually, at almost exactly the place where the trail started. There the Kaibab limestone gleams white in the sun a mile above one's head. At night a light can be seen glimmering there like a star. It was from thence one came and it is back there one must somehow manage to get.

The journey down has given a perspective, a sense of the magnitude of the phenomena, one cannot possibly get from the rim. On the other hand, the coziness of Phantom Ranch is deceptive again, because it conveys an exaggerated sense of the extent to which the Canyon has been tamed. One dropped over the rim, one persisted for a few hours along a perfectly practicable trail and one has arrived without incident or any great difficulty at the very bottom.

Actually, however, one has made merely a little foray along a carefully selected, long accustomed and carefully engineered route to a single spot. But it is only along the rim and along the river that the Canyon is known with any thoroughness to anyone. Many of the buttes have never, so far as is known, been climbed; many of the walls, plateaus, and side canyons have, so far as the record goes, never been visited. All about are hundreds of square miles of terra incognita. Only a few years ago Arizona Senator Barry Goldwater discovered by helicopter a great natural bridge in the Redwall which had not only never been visited but whose very existence was unknown. And another single incident will suggest even better the wildness and the difficulty of the terrain.

In 1944 two army pilots bailed out of a failing plane at eighteen thousand feet above the lights of the village. Instead of landing there, they watched the lights disappear over their heads and came to earth on what turned out to be the Tonto Plateau. After three days they were spotted by rescuers who dropped food by parachute. But it was five days before organized parties could reach them. One party descended from the south rim but presently found itself cut off by an uncrossable side canyon. Finally a party on the north rim spotted a rockfall down the Redwall which promised the possibility of a descent, and they finally reached the victims. Stray only a little from the marked trail, and you may find yourself unable to get back onto it again.

On their first night below, some travelers still sway with their mules, dream of precipices, or begin in anticipation the slow climb back. I found myself instead half-meditating and

Farther journey in more time

half-dreaming about those long departed seas which had
flowed in and then vanished; even more persistently of the
great mountain ranges which rose slowly and then, infinitely
more slowly, dissolved into sand and mud. How far from
solid is the solid ground beneath one's feet, and how far
from eternal are the eternal hills! Two Himalayas or Alps
had risen and vanished on the site of the Canyon before
life had got further than the protozoa and the jellyfish.

As soon as nature has made a mountain, she seems to regret it and she begins to tear it down. Then, once she has
torn it down, she makes another—perhaps, as here, precisely
where the former mountain had once towered. Speed the
action up as in those movies of an opening flower, and the
landscape of the earth would seem as insubstantial and
as phantasmagorial as the cloudscape of a thundery afternoon. "For a thousand years," said the Psalmist, "in thy
sight are but as yesterday." A thousand? Say rather a hundred million.

Rivers do the final work as they flow, more and more
slowly, through the canyons they have cut down to a lesser
and lesser gradient until they swing slowly back and forth
in a shifting meander which gradually wears away even
the minor hillocks and creates a featureless plain. This is
to me one of the less dramatic but one of the most impressive
of the geological processes, and I confess that I had never
been able to visualize it clearly until I spent an hour or two
looking out from an airplane flying at twelve thousand feet
above a typical "old" landscape—a flat plain bounded by low

hills fifty miles to the east and the west of the slow ineffectual-looking river which wound peacefully along. How, one first wonders, could so insignificant a stream be responsible for a flat valley a hundred miles in width?

Look at its present behavior and you can see. Notice, for instance, that point where it now flows against the side of a low hummock. Then look at the sandbank just opposite. Obviously the stream flowed quite recently where the sandbank now is. But as the channel silted up, the stream was thrown against the side of the hillock at whose base it now gnaws. Thus, in the course of a few thousand years, it swings in widening arcs back and forth until it flattens mile after mile of the broadening plain. "Peneplaining" is what the geologists call this process, and most of the wide, smiling vales of the earth have been thus made, though, at some still more distant day, some of them may again be lifted and broken into mountains just as that plain which had once been the Archean alps of the Grand Canyon region was lifted and broken anew to form the younger alps which had to be flattened in their turn before the Algonkian sediments could be deposited upon the plain they had again become.

How much longer will this cycle of mountain building and peneplaining go on? Will it repeat itself again here at the Canyon, which is so obviously already undergoing one of the first stages of transformation as water and ice are widening it? Will the river, still cutting deeper, tend to swing more widely as it slows down? Will it undermine the Canyon walls and, ultimately, wander slowly back and forth

Farther journey in more time

across a plain destined someday to become, perhaps, a sea
and then, after the sea has deposited a new layer of limestone, to be tossed up into a mighty mountain range once
more?

Something like this has happened more than once in the
past, though of course no one can know whether or for how
many times it will happen again. One set of forces is per-
petually engaged somewhere in reducing the surface of the
earth to the dead level of an almost featureless plain, and
such a featureless plain is everywhere the final stage—unless
it is heaved into mountains again or unless, as has frequently
happened, volcanic eruptions spew lava upon it. But our
earth is getting older. These successive levelings may be part
of a sort of running-down process. Presumably, as the globe
cools, the upheavals will become less frequent and less violent, though nobody knows for how many millions of years
(certainly for more than a billion) they have been going
on, or for how long they will continue. And yet, presumably
again, there will be an end to them when the heat pressures
have finally reached an equilibrium.

Thus these phenomena, though local on our earth, constitute a kind of "increasing entropy" roughly analogous
to the "running down" of the whole universe and its ultimate "heat death" which, a few years ago, was so confidently
predicted as inevitable by Sir James Jeans and others. The
sun cools, heat flows everywhere from hotter to cooler
places, thus tending to equalize all temperatures until, ultimately, the temperature will be the same everywhere, and

all energy will be in a stable equilibrium so that nothing can ever happen or change again. As one might put it too simply: Whatever goes up must come down, but it does not necessarily go up again.

Those who cannot anticipate with equanimity the death of the universe some billions of years hence may take heart from the fact that the most recent physical investigations have indicated that it is not running down as fast as was once thought. The sun is not merely burning; it is radioactive and not consuming itself nearly so fast as it would if it were no more than a ball of fire. The mysterious cosmic rays may be building energy up in unexpected places. The great clock of the universe may be at least partly self-winding or, in other words, there may be more life in the old boy than was once supposed. As the Cambridge cosmologist, E. A. Milne, wrote recently in more dignified language and with characteristic British calm when discussing large matters: "I am now convinced that an unconditional prediction of a heat-death for the universe is an over-statement."

Even the future leveling of the Grand Canyon may, then, be far from the end of the story. By the time some future geologist is studying the worn-down bases of the Rockies where they have been exposed by some canyon cut through thousands of feet of later sediments, the Archean rocks of the inner gorge of our Canyon may have been worn completely away or buried again deeper than they were buried when the Colorado first began to cut the strata which now overlay them.

Farther journey in more time

In the bright sun of morning Phantom Ranch's rocky dell looks solid enough, and the clear, cold water of Bright Angel Creek seems to justify Tennyson's rash assumption that brooks go on forever. Life-giving water has made a cheerful spot, isolated and self-contained; and because the intimate little hills and crags shut it in nearly everywhere and thus close the view, one can easily forget that its position is so peculiar and so inaccessible. It might well be the Happy Valley prison of some western Prince Rasselas brought up ignorant of any other world.

Those travelers who have no time because they must hurry on to some other place where also they will have no time are already mounting their mules for the climb back out, probably via the Kaibab Trail which will carry them to the rim at a point four miles east of that from which they started. It is chosen because, being somewhat shorter and a good deal steeper, the going up is easier on the riders, though harder on the mules which must stop every ten or fifteen minutes to catch their breath. The more leisurely visitors will stay a day, or two, or three, to enjoy the Happy Valley and to let some sense of their adventure sink in.

On the first of such days stiff knees and weary backs may well disincline them to do more than stroll the half mile down to the river just at the point where Bright Angel pours its crystal water into the sand- and silt-laden Colorado, there to test with a finger its icy temperature so different from that of the river's tepid water, and perhaps—if they are as lucky as I have been—to see a water ouzel or dipper bobbing on a stone. On succeeding days they may explore on foot or on muleback some of the innumerable nooks and enjoy the ever varying vistas provided by side canyons leading upward toward the invisible north rim. One surprising little oasis some five miles from the ranch they should not miss: Ribbon Falls, where one of the final tributaries of Bright Angel comes in from the west and creates a fantastic little dell of its own.

Obviously, the falls were once a hundred feet high. Now they are only about half as much, because they splash down upon the top of a truncated cone of limestone which has reached up to meet them half the distance they once fell. It is a stalagmite without a cave, gradually built up by the evaporation of lime-rich water and no doubt destined in time to close the gap entirely and thus to abolish the falls. For thirty or forty feet round about the air is damp with spray, and the spray has called into being a fernery most unexpected amid semidesert rocks. In a cranny of the cone itself Venus maidenhair flourishes and its surprising presence reminds one of the marvel of plant distribution, of the astonishing success which so many plants have had in discovering and colonizing the often restricted and isolated areas congenial to them—in this case an area of only a few square feet marooned in the middle of many miles of inhospitable territory.

For many plants and animals the Canyon is, as we shall presently notice, one of the most impassable of natural barriers. During thousands of years some have been unable to cross it and are to be found to the north or to the south but not on both sides. Yet here is the maidenhair, one of the crankiest of plants. It can grow only in very damp air and seldom anywhere except on limestone. Yet here, where an isolated spot provides just the right conditions, we find it.

The secret is, of course, the innumerable tiny, wind-borne spores it produces at the curled edge of its delicate leaves. They are scattered literally to all winds and they can be carried far. Billions must have fallen throughout the length and breadth of the Canyon as well as over the plateau it cuts. Billions must have lain useless over hundreds of square miles where they could never germinate, much less grow. But of those billions a few, perhaps only one, fell here; and because it did, the species has been flourishing below Ribbon Falls for no one can say how many years, perhaps before the cone began to rise to meet the falls as they tumble down. Many are called but few are chosen. To see this little miracle is by itself worth the journey down.

How difficult is that journey? The question is worth answering for the sake of the many who stand doubting on the rim as they catch a glimpse of a party threading its way across the face of some precipice thousands of feet below. Perhaps the best answer is simply that many people neither young nor especially accustomed to strenuous exercise do make it and are glad to have done so. Often they arrive very weary; sometimes their unaccustomed knees collapse under them when they are helped down from their mules. A few who are terrified by heights are quite unhappy for a few hours. But the fright, like the fatigue, is soon past and it leaves nothing behind. I have never heard anyone say he was sorry he had come. Perhaps the most usual reaction was summed up in what I heard from a middle-aged lady who had just been helped out of the saddle. "That wasn't too much," she said. And then, as her knees buckled, "But it was plenty."

6

The great unknown

While I dabbled my feet in the crystal water of Bright Angel Creek just where it mingles with the silt-laden Colorado— "too thick to drink, too thin to plow"—I was thinking of two things, one scientific, the other historical. The scientific had to do with the power of this great river to transport material.

At the moment it was at a very low stage and merely green with the silt which was all it could carry. At most places, however, the shore line was a rocky beach overlaid with well-worn stones, from egg to football size, which higher water had obviously once rolled along. Much more impressive still were huge boulders, tons in weight, in the stream itself. The disproportion between what the river could carry now and what it had obviously once carried seemed almost too great to credit. Most people, I think, are as astonished as I was to learn the law which the scene so vividly illustrates.

Roughly, so the geophysicists say, it is this: the transporting power of a given stream varies as the sixth power of its speed. Multiply two by itself five times and you get sixty-four. Multiply ten by itself five times and you get one million. In other words, a stream flowing at two miles per hour will carry a rock fragment sixty-four times as heavy as it could carry at one mile. If it flows at ten miles per hour, then it can move a fragment weighing a million times as much. In other words, the situation is a good deal like that of the customer in the ancient tale who was so incautious as to promise the blacksmith one penny for the first nail, two for the second, and so on. Dealing with rivers and their power to transport, you get very soon from the invisibly small particles the Colorado can transport at low water to the huge boulders it can roll along at high.

The historical fact I was simultaneously aware of is at least as interesting. I had got to the mouth of Bright Angel Creek without any danger, without too strenuous an effort, and in the course of what is only a routine expedition. Yet less than a hundred years ago the whole region was a real

The great unknown

terra incognita, and the name Bright Angel Creek was bestowed in 1869 by the first white man to stand where I stood. Moreover, he had come the long, hard route—in a twenty-foot wooden boat through innumerable dangerous, boulder-strewn rapids all the way from the frontier town of Green River, Wyoming, more than five hundred miles from Grand Canyon's eastern end.

When he started his perilous journey, the Canyon itself was hardly more than a rumor and much of the surrounding country quite unknown. The best maps of the region left completely blank a space varying from three hundred to five hundred miles long and from one hundred to two hundred miles broad. When he had finished his journey to the western end of the Canyon, the whole stretch of the river was part of both science and history, though twenty years were to pass before another man had the hardihood to repeat the journey.

Under the date, August 16, 1869, this first explorer, Major John Wesley Powell, wrote: "We must dry our rations again today, and make oars. The Colorado is never a clear stream, but for the past three or four days it has been raining much of the time, and the floods, which are pouring over the walls, have brought down great quantities of mud, making it exceedingly turbid now. The little affluent which we have discovered here, is a clear, beautiful creek or river, as it would be termed in this western country where streams are not abundant. We have named one stream away above, in

GRAND CANYON

honor of the Great Chief of the 'Bad Angels,' [Dirty Devil Creek] and as this is in beautiful contrast to that we conclude to name it 'Bright Angel.' "

Not far away he came upon "a mealing stone" and the foundations of two or three ancient Indian dwellings —proof enough that here, too, when we talk about "discovery" we mean only "by a white man." But the Indians who had built these houses had probably not come very far, and there is no evidence that any considerable number ever inhabited the depths of the Canyon.

In due time, Major Powell was to become a leading authority on the geography, geology, ethnology and potentialities of the southwestern region and, before he died, a sort of elder statesman. But at the moment he was only a nearly unknown, largely self-educated man who had organized the expedition with no more than a nod from the United States Government and a few small sums advanced by several different scientific organizations.

Born in New York State in 1834, Powell was the son of a Methodist minister who had moved westward into Illinois, and his early career was typical of a generation eager for education despite almost insuperable difficulties. He taught school from time to time to defray the expense of short stays at various small western schools; he attended Oberlin College briefly; and he worked his way into honorary or ill-paid positions with various minor scientific societies and museums. When the war came, he volunteered into the Union

The great unknown

Army and he left it minus one arm but with the rank of major. Then he taught natural science at the struggling Illinois Wesleyan University and with that position as a steppingstone got a small subsidy from a minor museum of natural history and from the United States Government the right to draw rations from army stores. Thus shakily supported, he set out with a group of twelve to explore the Rockies and to collect natural history specimens.

None of Powell's men had had much experience or training to fit them for the kind of work to be done, and after a summer of exploration plus five rugged months in winter quarters the original party disintegrated. Powell, however, was by now determined upon his bolder project. He returned to Washington and again got no more than the right to draw rations and to convert some of the allowance into cash. To his order and after his design three heavy, twenty-one-foot wooden boats each capable of carrying 4,500 pounds (also one smaller pilot boat) were built and shipped to the town of Green River, Wyoming, then the railroad terminus. There Powell organized a new party consisting of five "mountain men" (i.e., trappers), his brother Walter, and three other volunteers—none with much experience or scientific training. His plan was to spend some ten months in the Canyon.

No one, it should be repeated, knew much of anything about either the Grand Canyon itself or the hundreds of miles of canyons and rapids which lay between his starting point and the beginning of what was then known only vaguely as "the big canyon." Rumor had it that there the river dropped in falls higher than Niagara and for long distances ran underground. Indians told Powell how the Canyon had been opened by the gods to provide passage for a sorrowing chief to visit his dead wife in the happier land to which she had been translated, and they warned him against the impiety of trying to pass through it. For all anyone knew, he and his party might be heading for inevitable death.

While the final preparations were being made on the banks of the Green River, the eastern and western ends of the first transcontinental railroad were joined, and the first train to cross the bridge rumbled over Powell's head. Finally, just after noon on May 24, 1869, the boats shoved off. Nothing more was heard of the adventurers as week after week passed, and the newspapers reported that the entire party had been lost in rapids not far below the starting point. Finally, however, Powell left a letter dated July 17, or nearly two months after the start, at a little settlement near the junction of the Green and Yampa Rivers in northern Utah.

The party had been having its troubles but was learning fast. Dangerous water was encountered almost immediately. In fact, a solitary foolhardy adventurer named John Hood who set out alone two days before Powell promptly drowned not far from Green River, and his death was probably responsible for the rumor that the Powell party had been lost. The early difficulties were nothing to what Powell was to meet later but they provided relatively easy problems to be solved by a developing technique. Powell himself scouted ahead in the light boat. Often it was necessary to unload the others completely and to let them down on ropes as far as possible before turning them loose. Some of the supplies and instruments were soon lost in these operations, but on July 6 the expedition left camp near the mouth of the Uinta River and entered the real unknown.

Uranium hunters have recently opened up this part of Utah somewhat; but even a decade ago it was still as empty an area as any in the United States, and in 1869 it was almost completely unknown. On July 16 the voyagers reached the point where the Grand River joins the Green to make the Colorado and where three canyons, each half a mile deep, come together. During the two months past they had seen a white man only once; their food was low; attempts at hunting and fishing had been largely failures. Camping on a spot that probably no white man had ever seen, they were already, by Powell's computation, 538 miles from the starting point. Then on July 21 they started down the rushing river where the rapids were so dangerous that often the boats could no longer be "lined" but had to be "portaged" empty along the banks. Fortunately, no one knew that at many points in Grand Canyon the walls would rise so directly from the water's edge that there would be no possible passage by foot so that men and boats together would have, willy-nilly, to "shoot" the rapids.

By August 4 they had reached a point just above the site of the present Navajo Bridge and a little later camped where the Little Colorado empties into the Colorado, and Grand

Canyon proper begins, its walls already rising three thousand feet above the river. The morale of the company was by no means what it should have been. For one thing, the flour and bacon upon which they chiefly depended was moldy and in short supply. For another, the "mountain men" were impatient with what they regarded as the unnecessary delays caused by Powell's insistence upon attempting to fix their position by astronomical observation. Nevertheless, they all stuck by the group for the present, and Powell himself never faltered. A stretch of absolutely unknown river, running for no one knew how many miles through an equally unknown canyon, lay before them. The distance to safety was in fact approximately two hundred miles, and for long stretches the walls which enclosed the river were unclimbable. Unless they got through to the end, the chances of coming out alive were small, and Powell was indulging in no mere rhetoric when he wrote in his report:

"We are now ready to start on our way down the Great Unknown. Our boats, tied to a common stake, are chaffing each other, as they are tossed by the fretful river. They ride high and buoyant, for their loads are lighter than we could desire. We have but a month's rations remaining. The flour has been resifted through the mosquito net sieve; the spoiled bacon has been dried, the worst of it boiled; the few pounds of dried apples have been spread in the sun, and reshrunken to their normal bulk; the sugar has all melted, and gone on its way down the river; we have a huge sack of coffee.

The great unknown

The lightening of the boats has this advantage: they will ride the waves better, and we have but little to carry when we make a portage.

"We are three quarters of a mile in the depths of the earth, and the great river shrinks into insignificance, as it dashes its angry waves against the walls and cliffs, that rise to the world above . . .

"We have an unknown distance yet to run; an unknown river yet to explore. What falls there are, we know not; what rocks beset the channel we know not; what walls rise over the river, we know not."

Presently the temperature reached 115 degrees and there were few camping places. The walls which pressed so narrowly upon the river that no portage was possible rose a mile high above it. Capsizings and duckings were an everyday occurrence, and the water-soaked food was spoiling. The bacon had to be thrown away; the leavening for the bread was lost. On August 11 Bradley, a diary-keeping member of the party, wrote:

> If Major does not do something soon I fear the consequences, but he is content and seems to think that biscuits made of sour and musty flour and a few dried apples is ample to sustain a laboring man. If he can only study geology he will be happy without food or shelter but the rest of us are not afflicted with it to an alarming extent.

Powell's own report covering approximately the same period illustrates Bradley's sour comment:

GRAND CANYON

The walls now are more than a mile in heighth . . . A thousand feet of this is up through granite crags, then steep slopes and perpendicular cliffs rise, one above another, to the summit. The gorge is black and narrow below, red and grey and flaring above with crags and angular projections on the walls, which, cut in many places by side canyons, seem to be a vast wilderness of rocks. Down in these grand, gloomy depths we glide, ever listening, for the mad waters keep up their roar; ever watching, ever peering ahead, for the narrow canyon is winding, and the river is closed in so that we can see but a few hundred yards and what there may be below we know not; but we listen for falls, and watch for rocks, or stop now and then, in a bay or recess, to admire the gigantic scenery.

By August 25 the party had come nearly two hundred miles from the mouth of the Little Colorado and was near the end of the Canyon where the country opens up and human habitation was not far away. They did not, however, know how close they were to safety, and only five days' rations remained. Just ahead lay what appeared to be the most difficult rapids they had yet encountered. In fact, they seemed impossible and there was no room for a portage. The walls might or might not be climbable but even if they proved to be so, the nearest known settlement to the north was many miles away across the unknown plateaus and deserts which stretched away from the rim.

Powell considered the situation carefully and decided that the only chance of getting through was by "lining" the boats down the first fall, running the rapids to the second, and then rowing furiously to avoid being dashed against a great rock in the stream. It was the darkest day of the trip, and for the first time some members of the party refused to follow their leader.

O. G. Howland, perhaps the best educated man of the group, proposed that they should all attempt to climb out. Powell refused, but Howland, Howland's brother and a certain Bill Dun took two rifles and a shotgun, leaving Powell and the rest to take their chances with what Powell was to name "Separation Rapids." Wrote Bradley: "The three boys stood on the cliff looking at us and having waved adieu we dashed through the next rapid and then into an eddy where we stopped to catch our breath and bail out the water from our sunken boats. We never had such a rapid before but we have run a worse one this afternoon." When the rapids had been safely run, a gun was fired in the hope that the three deserters might hear it and return. But there was no response.

Six and a half miles below Separation Rapids was another very bad stretch of angry water—but it was the last. On the thirtieth of August the party had reached open country. Three Mormons and an Indian were encountered. Powell was again in what might be called "known country." In fact, just eleven years before, Lieutenant J. C. Ives had come *up* the river from Yuma beyond this point. In his diary Bradley wrote: "All that we regret now is that the three boys who took to the mountains are not here to share our joy and triumph." Powell, writing up his experiences somewhat later, strikes the same note.

"Ever before us has been an unknown danger, heavier than immediate peril. Every waking hour passed in the Grand Canyon has been one of toil. We have watched with deep solicitude the steady disappearance of our scant supply of rations, and from time to time have seen the river snatch a portion of the little left, while we were ahungered. And danger and toil were endured in those gloomy depths, where ofttimes the clouds hid the sky by day, and but a narrow zone of stars could be seen at night. Only during the few hours of deep sleep, consequent on hard labor, has the roar of waters been hushed. Now the danger is over; now the toils have ceased; now the gloom has disappeared; now the firmament is bounded only by the horizon; and what a vast expanse of constellations can be seen.

"The river rolls by us in silent majesty; the quiet of the camp is sweet; our joy is almost ecstasy. We sit till long after midnight, talking of the grand canyon, talking of home, but chiefly talking of the three men, who left us. Are they wandering in those depths, unable to find a way out? Are they searching over desert lands above the water, or are they already nearing the settlements?"

What he did not know at the time of reaching safety was that the three who made the wrong decision were to pay the penalty for it. Somehow or other they managed to climb out of the Canyon but only to be murdered by Indians—under circumstances which have never been quite clear.

The great unknown

Powell, who had been nobody when he left Green River and barely able to win a small gesture of assistance from the national government, went back to Washington a hero. He had done a great deal more than merely run a difficult river that had never been traversed before. He had improvised the method by which the feat was to be accomplished again and, sketchy as were both his equipment and his training, he had a keen enough scientific eye to grasp the meaning of what he saw and to confirm the opinion of an earlier geologist who had seen only the lower end of the Canyon.

Such a canyon could, as Powell clearly explained, have been formed in only one way: by the slow elevation of strata through which the river cut as the strata rose. "Thus it is that the study of the structural characters of the valley and canyons teaches . . . the relation between progress and upheaval and that of erosion and corrosion, showing that these latter were pari passu with the former." Perhaps the simplest summary of Powell's achievement is to say that in the course of a few weeks he turned a rumor into a fact by filling in one of the last remaining blank spaces on the map of the United States and that he had, at the same time, turned a legend into a chapter of geology. Fittingly, he also fixed the nomenclature. Before his journey the usual phrase was "the big canyon." Ever since it has been what Powell called it: "Grand Canyon."

The expedition had no photographer and no artist so it could bring back no pictures, and as Wallace Stegner points

out in his *Beyond the Hundredth Meridian*, the first attempts
to draw or paint the Canyon are little more than "pictures of
the artist's dismay." What is probably the earliest, by a certain Baron von Egloffstein who had accompanied the 1857
Ives expedition upriver to the beginning of the Canyon's
western end, looks more like something out of Doré's *Inferno*
than like Arizona—a narrow cleft in sheer topless walls which
might pass as a surrealist's interpretation of claustrophobia.
Another picture by the same artist and the first purporting
to represent any part of the main Canyon is thus aptly
described by Stegner: "Nothing here is realistic: stratification is ignored, forms are wildly seen, narrowness and depth
are wildly exaggerated, the rocks might as well be of the texture of clouds." But artists' interpretations rapidly improved.
A chromolithograph published in the seventies and probably based on a photograph taken from near the rim shows
the stratification plainly, and accurately represents the pro-
file. Not many years later the painter, Thomas Moran, made
a trip in Powell's company from Salt Lake to the north rim
and did a painting based at least partly on his own observation. Hung in the Capitol at Washington it gave many
Americans their first accurate notion of what their country's
greatest natural wonder really looks like.

Shortly after his return to Washington Powell was
granted ten thousand dollars for continued explorations of
the West. On May 22, 1871, he was off from Green River
again with a new, somewhat better organized and equipped
expedition. The river was charted as the party proceeded,

and photographs were taken with a cumbersome wet-plate camera weighing, with its necessary accessories, more than a ton. By August 24 the Canyon proper had been reached, but it was not again traversed. Powell had other plans for what he regarded as more useful work. To the geological, geographic, ethnological and economic study of the West he was to devote many years.

Though Powell had shown that the Canyon could be conquered and that there were no underground passages or Niagaralike falls, no one seemed anxious to repeat his journey. In fact, twenty years were to pass before Robert Brewster Stanton, a surveyor looking for a railway route, became the second leader to run the whole course of the river. Three of his party were drowned in Marble Canyon above the mouth of the Little Colorado but, after refitting, he and the other members of his group reached the Gulf of California on April 26, 1890. Other adventurers followed at long intervals: George F. Flavell and one companion (probably prospectors or trappers) in 1896; Nathan Galloway, also with one companion, in 1897; two prospectors, Charles Russell and E. R. Mommette, in 1907. Julius F. Stone, apparently the first of the gentlemen adventurers, set out in company with the experienced Galloway and a photographer, reaching Needles in 1909.

Accumulating experience and improved equipment were gradually making the journey a little less hazardous, and in 1911 another epoch was opened when the brothers Emory

and E. L. Kolb, professional photographers who had spent
ten years exploring parts of the Canyon from the rim downward, left Green River with two boats and a movie camera
on September 8 and arrived at Bright Angel Creek on November 16. They climbed the trail to what was by then a tourist
center on the south rim, returned to the river on December
19, and reached Needles on January 18, 1912. The film which
they made has been seen by many thousands of visitors to
the Canyon and is still shown at their studio not far from
the hotel on the south rim. Finally, in 1938, Norman
Nevills, young son of a prospector settled at Mexican Hat,
Utah, on the San Juan River some miles above its junction
with the Colorado, designed new boats, learned new techniques and made the trip through the Canyon by river as
near an everyday (or at least every-year) affair as it is
likely ever to be. He was killed in an airplane a few years
later, but the sufficiently adventurous can now accompany
routinely organized expeditions along the whole route which
Powell pioneered.

Meanwhile, the transformation of a portion of the rim
from a terra incognita into one of the most frequently visited
of tourist attractions proceeded even more rapidly. Distinguished visitors—including John Muir and John Burroughs,
the two best known publicists for the natural beauties of
America—drew increasing attention to the region, and
when Theodore Roosevelt camped for a while in 1903, just
on the spot where presentday visitors to the depths spend

the night at Phantom Ranch, he was among the last who could claim to be doing anything very unusual. In 1908 he proclaimed Grand Canyon a national monument and in 1919 Congress created it a national park—as Muir had suggested years before that it should be and as Roosevelt had urged. The present bridge across the river at the foot of Bright Angel Trail was built in 1928 to replace the swaying structure which had been stretched across in 1921 when the still earlier cable car was abandoned.

The elder Roosevelt is a controversial political figure. Even as conservationist he provokes from some the objection that his activities as a sportsman who condoned trophy-collecting were somewhat inconsistent with his professed desire to protect wildlife. But it should never be forgotten that no other man in a position of political power ever did so much to preserve something of America's wild heritage. On the occasion of his trip to the Canyon he made a speech in the course of which he said:

> In the grand Canyon, Arizona has a natural wonder which so far as I know, is in kind absolutely unparalleled throughout the rest of the world. I want to ask you to do one thing in connection with it in your own interest and in the interest of the country—to keep this great wonder of nature as it now is. I was delighted to learn of the wisdom of the Santa Fe railroad people in deciding not to build their hotel on the brink of the Canyon. I hope you will not have a building of any kind, not a summer cottage, a hotel or anything else, to mar the wonderful grandeur, the sublimity, the great loveli-

ness and beauty of the Canyon. Leave it as it is. You can not improve on it. The ages have been at work on it, and man can only mar it. What you can do is to keep it for your children, your children's children, and for all who come after you, as one of the great rights which every American if he can travel at all should see. We have gotten past the stage, my fellow citizens, when we are to be pardoned if we treat any part of our country as something to be skinned for two or three years for the use of the present generation, whether it be the forest, the water, the scenery. Whatever it is, handle it so that your children's children will get the benefit of it.

Reading this only a little more than a half a century later and remembering some of the things that have happened since, one may be tempted to sour comments. Equally disturbing thoughts can arise if one looks back rather than forward from Theodore Roosevelt's time. Less than thirty-five years before he spoke, the whole region around about had been something unknown waiting to be discovered. Yet so rapidly do we move from the unknown to the known and then to the exploited and the devastated, that a mere thirty-five years after Powell had become a hero of exploration it had already become necessary to take steps to prevent Powell's remote wilderness from being laid waste by those already beginning to swarm in and destroy it.

7

Thus far shalt thou go

Cárdenas, the first white man ever to approach the Canyon, spent five or six days trying to find his way down into it and then turned back in despair. Unknowingly, he was doing only what many different animals—and for that matter, many plants—had been doing before him during thousands of years. Thus the Canyon is, among many other things, one of the most effective of the barriers which shut off one habitable area of the earth's surface from another.

Few mountain ranges are as effective, because they seldom stretch for so long a distance without a pass through which the persistent can make their way. And though even the Canyon once had (toward the shallower east end, where climbing is possible) a ford known as Horse Thief Ford because of the stolen horses led to safety from Utah to Arizona or vice versa, this was the only crossing known. And only a horse thief would risk it.

Even today, when good roads lead the long way around both ends, the Canyon still functions as a physical as well as a psychological barrier between human as well as natural communities. The region to the north, commonly known as "the Strip," is cut off from the rest of Arizona and is nearly empty. The few scattered inhabitants came mostly, like the flora and fauna, from Utah to the north, and they are so isolated that a little band of heretic Mormons could establish at Short Creek an independent community where they practiced exuberant polygamy and in general defied the authority of the national government for years until in 1953 a raiding party (dubiously justifiable, as many thought) broke it up.

Man, being the most mobile of animals and also the only one to have developed a science of logistics, has by now flowed around the ends of the Canyon and so, though he still rarely crosses the barrier, he has mingled with his fellows on the opposite side. On the other hand, some plants and animals have never crossed the barrier at all, and the Canyon marks the limit of their distribution, northward or southward as the case may be. They cannot make their way, not even slowly in the course of generations, down one side

Thus far shalt thou go

and up the other, because the journey would carry them through regions where for one reason or another—unsuitable climate, lack of the accustomed food or what not—they cannot survive. They must turn back even as Cárdenas did.

The most striking and best known example of two closely related animals which, for many thousands of years, have been kept separate by the Canyon is that of the Kaibab and the Abert squirrels which happen to be the handsomest representatives of their family in the United States and likely to win admiring attention from any traveler who sees either the one or the other, even though he knows nothing of their story.

Both are large, noticeably larger than the eastern gray squirrel. Both also have rich, reddish-brown backs, handsome ear tufts or tassels which appear only in winter and huge fluffy tails providing a panache extravagant even for a squirrel. But they are also strikingly different. The Abert has a white belly and a grayish tail; the Kaibab a black belly and an astonishing pure white plume behind. The first is the commoner, occurring in isolated but favorable mountain areas south of the Canyon and scattered over both the Southwestern United States and northern Mexico. The Kaibab is restricted to an island plateau some twenty by forty miles in extent, which is the northern half of the dome through which the Canyon is cut and which is isolated, not only by the Canyon to the south, but by deserts to the east, and west and the north. In that restricted area he is by no means uncommon. Sometimes he is seen around the north rim camp grounds, though in my experience the surest place to see him for either aesthetic or scientific reasons, is in the great forest of pines at Jacob Lake, through which all visitors headed for the north rim must pass.

The habits of the Abert and the Kaibab are essentially identical, and both are restricted vertically as well as horizontally. All live in the region of high pines at six to eight thousand feet, making only rare forays a short distance down to the live-oak region or a short distance up to the firs. Sometimes they inhabit tree holes but mostly they build bushel-sized homes of leaves lined with grass or bark and put high in the trees where, in bad weather, the inhabitants may stay for a week or ten days at a time. They have the engaging habit of transporting their young under their bellies, tail between their forelegs and with the baby holding on for dear life. They store little food, and though they sometimes rummage around the ground for seeds and tubers, they are wholly dependent for their main food supply on the living inner bark of the pine tree—principally the ponderosa. In winter they climb out to the ends of small branches, cut them off, and then, on the ground, gnaw through to the nourishing layer where life is still going on.

More or less omnivorous animals can range widely. Those confined to a special diet are naturally confined to the regions where it can be found and they are always to some extent in danger. If something cuts off their essential food, they are doomed and at best they are closely restricted to regions where it is obtainable. The Australian koala, which eats only the leaves of the eucalyptus, is a notable example, and some believe that the disappearance of the passenger pigeon was less the result of wholesale slaughter by man than of the fact that he was so largely dependent upon the fruit of the beech tree. Certainly the odd history of the two tassel-eared squirrels has been wholly determined by the fact that they are "obligated," as the ecologists say, to the tall pines. They cannot leave the regions where they happen to have been born, because such regions are separated by the to them impassable deserts and by canyon bottoms. Hence, the northerners and the southerners have been prevented from intermarriage for so long that they have evolved into different races.

Probably—though fossil evidence is lacking—a single race once occupied pretty much the whole area from northern Mexico up into Utah. Then the Rockies were lifted and, slightly later, about the beginning of the Pleistocene, the ranges in southern Arizona. This means that something like a million years ago the lowlands began to be transformed into deserts. During the succeeding ice ages the region was cold, but as it warmed up about 35,000 years ago, aridity and heat drove the pines higher and higher into the mountains, and the squirrels were compelled to follow them. Hence, neither the pine nor the squirrel is now commonly found at less than eight thousand feet elevation. Thus little communities of squirrels were cut off, one from another, with no avenue of communication open, and interbreeding, which cancels out the heritable variations plants and animals alike tend to develop, became impossible.

Much more ancient history furnishes, of course, more spectacular examples of what happens when certain plants or animals are isolated for long periods. When the white man first came to Australia, there were no mammals other than primitive marsupials except for bats, rats and a wild dog, all of which could have crossed the water either on their own wings, on floating logs, or in the boats with the aboriginal human colonizers. Still more striking is the fact that when white men first came to New Zealand, there were not even marsupials. And the explanation of both phenomena seems clear. Australia was cut off from the other main continental masses by a salt estranging sea before any mammals other than the marsupial had been developed; New Zealand at a still earlier period. But the less striking case of the tassel-eared squirrel is especially interesting, both because the isolation by mountain and canyon and desert is so much less immediately obvious than isolation by sea, and even more, just because the fact that it is so recent delights evolutionists by giving them an example of a very first step in, to use Darwin's famous phrase, "the origin of species."

Are the Kaibab and Abert squirrels different species or still merely "varieties"? C. Hart Merriam, who first described the Kaibab squirrel, called it a different species. Some of the present-day classifiers disagree. But there is not really much point in the dispute. The term "different species" had a very definite meaning before the doctrine of evolution was generally accepted. It meant a kind of plant or animal which had always been different from every other from the day of its "special creation." But since we have come to assume that all animals have evolved from common ancestors, and since every degree of differentiation exists between certain kinds, there is no objective criterion for determining what distinguishes a "species" from a "variety" and it is largely a matter of opinion. Either the two squirrels are well-marked varieties or they are just barely distinct species. You may take your choice. Edwin McKee puts the situation thus: "We appear to have here . . . a fine example of evolution in its first stages, not yet well defined in its trends and not yet in operation for a very long period, but having definite opportunities to develop well isolated forms along independent lines."

Of course, students of evolution would be even happier if they could point to some unmistakable way in which the difference between the two squirrels conferred upon each a positive "survival value" in his special environment. Did "natural selection" tend to favor a northern race with white tails? The best guess that anyone has been able to come up with is this: There is much snow where the Kaibab squirrel lives, much less in most of the Abert's range. And since both habitually carry their tails over their backs, a white tail would help camouflage its owner on snow-covered ground.

Farfetched? Perhaps. Variations do exist even when they

have no obvious survival value. Perhaps the differences between the coloration of the two squirrels helps them to survive in their different environments no more than the difference between an Alabama accent and that of a down-
Easterner constitutes adaptation to their environments. But
on the other side it may be pointed out that various northern animals—the snowshoe rabbit, for example—do turn
white in the season of snow and that the advantage seems
clear. Or, going back to the other side again, we may ask
why didn't both squirrels adapt to a less restricted diet
which would probably have been a good deal more ad-
vantageous to the race than white tails are?

Here, in other words, is another example of the fact that
evolution is not as simple, as clear, and as perfectly understood as is sometimes assumed. It does take place, and the
natural selection of useful variations does also take place.
But there are fundamental questions as well as questions of
detail which still have to be asked. Nearly everybody will
agree that organisms have not always tended to provide just
those variations which are potentially most useful. The Kaibab squirrel did not vary his diet, though he did change the
color of his tail, and possibly natural selection did enable
him to take advantage of that variation even though it may
have originated merely by chance. Some—perhaps an increasing number but still a minority—would also agree that
though the mechanical selection from among chance variations may account for the different tails on the two kinds
of tassel-eared squirrels, it is not so certainly by itself suf-

ficient to account for, say, the cooperation of the yucca moth with the yucca, the complicated techniques of the agricultural ant, or the seeming wisdom of those Australian birds who so carefully regulate the temperature in the incubators they build in lieu of brooding nests.

Nature seems to love variety—perhaps, as the mechanists would say, because the more different kinds of creatures there are, the more niches can be inhabited; perhaps because, like Thoreau, she would just like to have as many different kinds of men (and animals and plants and bugs) as possible. Perhaps she is still experimenting to see just how different she can make the two squirrels; and unless she, or man himself, breaks down the barrier before the experiment is complete, they may be even more interesting to some future evolutionist than they are now. As usual, however, she will take her time while even the most interested of us find it impossible to wait.

The great barrier of the Canyon itself is only one of the many things which make the whole region one of the most astonishingly varied in America or, for that matter, anywhere else. Within a rectangle some two hundred miles long and a hundred miles broad there are differences of altitude totaling more than ten thousand feet and climates varying from the subtropical to the arctic. There are low, flat, burning deserts; there is a mighty river, and there are dark, volcanic peaks reaching nearly thirteen thousand feet above sea level. Scenically, one may pass in less than an hour from one world to another which seems totally unrelated and pass at the same time from shirt sleeves to overcoat.

The geological "when" and "why" of this is another story and one that reaches down to a time, not very long before the first white man came, when some of the newest rock in the world was spewed out over an area next door to some of the most ancient anywhere exposed. But the biological consequences of this variety are obvious to any traveler who passes.

What he notices will depend upon the nature and extent of his interests, but unless he has accustomed himself so completely to an artificial environment that he has no awareness whatever of the natural world, he will notice something: perhaps only the difference between the arid desert and the pine-clad summits; perhaps, if he is interested in plants, the transition from alpine meadows to temperate oak, to cactus and creosote bush; perhaps, if he notices birds, the huge crested jays of the high woods which give place so soon to the desert sparrows and the sage thrashers of the hot flatlands. And whatever aspect of the changing scene he may take note of, it is part of a larger picture in which geology, climate, vegetation and animal life are all linked together. The forests are there because of the mountains and the jays because of the pines.

Merriam's contemporary, Ernst Haeckel, invented the term "ecology" (literally "housekeeping") to describe that new science which was to the plant and animal communi-

ties what "economics" is to human societies. Of course, naturalists had long known that Siberia was too cold for lions
and that marsh plants couldn't live in the desert, but while
they were busy for a century or two classifying and naming
the inhabitants of the earth and then a little later busy with
anatomy and physiology, they had made relatively little attempt to understand the complicated web of interrelations
which controls the flora and fauna of any region and establishes a balance which is often so delicate that either a
slight change in physical condition or the failure or success
of some one element contributing to the balance can set
off a series of changes which may have enormous consequences for man himself—especially when he is the one who
interferes with the balance.

Merriam himself was one of the earliest American Ecologists to make important contributions to the new science,
and it is no wonder that it was his survey of the Canyon region, made originally for the United States Government,
which suggested to him one of ecology's most important con-
cepts, namely that of life zones. Because so many of these
zones—as many as there are at sea level from Mexico to beyond the Arctic Circle—are so dramatically crowded together within the Canyon rectangle, they forced themselves
upon his attention.

This concept of life zones is based upon the fact that climate is one of the most obvious of the things which determine the range, not merely of this or that particular plant
or animal, but of an association or community of plants and

animals dependent upon one another as well as upon the climate. These plants and animals often compete; but they are also often necessary to one another—sometimes reciprocally, sometimes, as in the striking case of the tassel-eared squirrel and the pine, merely in a one-sided dependence. Thus a stable community is established in which even sworn enemies sometimes cannot prosper without one another as when, say, foxes depend upon mice as an essential part of their diet while, if there were no foxes, the unchecked growth of the mouse population would drive them to exhaust their food supply, perhaps to exterminate their food plants, and finally themselves succumb to disease or starvation. But once a balance is established, the community tends to remain in stable equilibrium until something upsets it— sometimes man's intervention, sometimes a catastrophic event like the rearing of the mountains which destroyed the pine squirrel community over a large part of what had once been its territory and thus prepared the way for other communities, including those in the hot desert.

If the earth were flat, then the climatic zones would correspond more or less with the geographical. We would have a Tropical belt, a Subtropical, and so on to the Arctic. But since altitude bears a relation to climate just as definite as that of latitude, there is no such correspondence, and you may even have, as you do in Arizona, an Arctic life zone near the top of the San Francisco Mountains and a Subtropical at the bottom of the Canyon or at Cameron, barely fifty miles from the mountain's Arctic.

Thus far shalt thou go

Of course, some factors besides altitude and latitude affect climate. For instance, the slopes of the two sides of a valley may lie in different life zones just because the sun shines longer on the one side than on the other. Moreover, identical temperature zones in widely separated regions of the earth do not always have identical plant-animal communities because, for one thing, moisture and the character of the soil favor or inhibit the organisms which might otherwise be at home there. Thus, there is a community appropriate to, say, an arid Subtropical and another to a moist Subtropical. Then, too, certain plants and animals have never colonized some suitable areas, because barriers formed by seas or mountains or deserts prevented their migration. Thus, there are neither koalas nor native eucalyptus trees upon which they could feed in the Northern Hemisphere, but the eucalyptus flourishes wonderfully when introduced into southern California, and so might the koala if animals with which it cannot compete (including man!) were not already established.

Such facts are of immense importance to man who introduced plants and animals into zones suited to them, as for instance when he took sheep to Australia—where there had been no large native mammals except the marsupials—or to South America. Even more important, perhaps, is the history of food plants, many of which were once local forms, sometimes perhaps local accidents, later intentionally transplanted to other suitable zones. And it is a curious fact that in almost every instance—as in the case of wheat, Indian corn, tobacco, bananas, sweet potatoes, etc., etc.—the present centers of most flourishing production are rather far removed from the place of origin, though they are in a corresponding life zone. Bananas, for example, came to Central America from Asia via Africa and the Canary Islands.

Because so many factors besides temperature influence a plant-animal community, present-day ecologists usually substitute a more complicated system than Merriam's for the classification of environments. But within a relatively limited area like the western half of the American continent his concept is very workable and enlightening.

Merriam recognized seven sharply distinguishable zones on the American continent ranging from the Tropical to the Arctic. On the eastern seaboard where there are no great variations in altitude you have to travel from Key West (just barely within the Tropical) all the way to northern Maine to pass through five of them. But in the West, where such tremendous differences in altitude occur within a few miles, the traveler is constantly passing from one zone to another and then back again.

Go up any steep slope, and you pass in a matter of hours through worlds which in the East are days apart; and the steeper the slope, the narrower the bands which fall within each zone. The most famous case of such narrow banding is the eastern slope of Mount San Jacinto just above Palm Springs, California, where the nearly ten-thousand-foot peak rises in just three airline miles eight thousand feet above the desert and so compresses within those three miles six of

Thus far shalt thou go

the seven life zones. Mounting, the traveler passes in a matter of minutes from one plant-animal community to another, and many organisms are confined sharply to their narrow band or layer. To get an equal variety on the eastern seaboard, you would have to go from central Florida to northern Canada.

Many trees, like the oak and the large pines, are found in their appropriate zones on each side of the continent. Other plants and also animals are characteristic of the East or West only, so that there is, for example, no sage brush in the East. Because of these differences caused by variations in the amount of moisture and other differences, special local names are now given to some of the western zones to distinguish them from the corresponding eastern zones. What, for instance, is called Austral in the East is called Sonoran in the West to indicate that though they correspond in temperature, they differ sharply in that the Sonoran is extremely arid. The communities flourishing within any of the western zones are, on the other hand, remarkably like those in a corresponding zone far away and equally unlike those of another zone which may be geographically next door. This is so generally true that Merriam recognized various "indicator" plants and animals—organisms, that is, which by themselves would serve to identify the zone and to all but guarantee the presence of others normally part of the same community.

Each of the six zones within the Canyon rectangle is thus sharply distinguished. In the Lower Sonoran (or Subtropical) the characteristic plants include the greasewood (Atriplex), Mormon tea (Ephedra), one of the yuccas and various cacti. There are also many lizards, pocket mice, and kangaroo rats but only a few birds—especially desert sparrows and sage thrashers. Just a little higher into the Upper Sonoran, evergreen oaks become the dominant tree, often mixed as they are on the south rim of the Canyon, with the small piñon pine. Here the piñon jay and the rock squirrel abound. But at about seven thousand feet the Transition zone begins, the ponderosa pine flourishes and the tassel-eared squirrel is an indicator animal. At about nine thousand, the Canadian zone begins, and the Douglas fir tends to replace the pine. Here the chickaree or spruce squirrel also appears. Another thousand feet up in the Hudsonian zone the fir persists but spruce appears; and under the trees more northerly herbaceous plants like the columbine and the pyrola grow profusely, Clark's crow is a dominant bird, and the porcupine a prevalent animal. Finally, at twelve thousand feet or so, as at the summit of San Francisco Peak, one is definitely within the Arctic zone, and while standing in a meadow sprinkled with flowers which also grow within the Arctic Circle, one may look down upon a Subtropical desert.

This Arctic meadow is nearly two thousand miles from the Arctic Circle. It is also more than 250 miles from the nearest peak reaching into its zone. The golden eagle raises its young there, and Merriam was delighted to discover a

Thus far shalt thou go

number of plants which Greely had brought back from Lady
Franklin Bay north of the northernmost part of Greenland
and not many degrees from the pole.

Here, they are growing within a very small area from
which they cannot possibly escape and at least 250 miles
from other members of their species. How did they get there
in the first place? Only one explanation seems possible and
it is that the Arctic flora advanced southward in front of the
glaciers during the great ice age. Then, as the glaciers retreated and the climate warmed, they took refuge higher
and higher into the cool mountains until only the tips of the
highest peaks were to them habitable. Should the world
grow much warmer (and there is some evidence that it is
warming up), they may disappear from even the San Francisco Peaks. If it should grow colder first, they will probably descend down the sides of the mountain, replacing the
plants which now occupy these lower slopes but which
could not stand the temperature the Arctic plants flourish
in.

After I had made in one day the billion-year journey
from the Archean rocks to the rim, the fancy struck me to
make in another the journey in latitude from Subtropical to
Arctic. Visually it is even more striking, because one *sees*
rather than merely *knows about* what one is doing, and
thanks to that dubious boon, the automobile, it can be made
in a mere matter of hours. From the Canyon rim the Arctic

peak is plainly visible, but to reach it one must first descend to the Subtropics from the Upper Sonoran zone in which the rim lies.

Strike eastward, and the road, which keeps close to the rim for many miles, carries you down the slope of a dome-shaped Kaibab Plateau and consequently past a canyon growing steadily shallower. At one point you may see in the distance the small canyon of the Little Colorado near where it joins the big canyon of the Colorado itself. Presently one is following the Little Colorado, cutting through country now definitely desert, and before long one reaches the crossroads at Cameron, an Indian post and gas station, all but lost in a flat sandy desert some three thousand feet lower than the south rim and so desperately arid that it is almost bare of vegetation.

To the south and now a little nearer at hand the dark mountains reach up, and if one takes the road running toward them, the ground surface changes from red-sandy to dead-black because its surface is a porous lava spewed out from these same mountains, all of which are volcanic cones and quite recent—in fact, the most recent large-scale phenomena of the whole region. One, called Sunset Crater, can be definitely dated as having been cast up less than a thousand years ago into a region then inhabited by man of a fairly advanced culture. The highest peak is somewhat earlier but of an age measured in thousands of years. It was once perhaps three thousand feet higher than now but it still rises 12,611 feet above sea level or five thousand above the

Thus far shalt thou go

plateau through which it burst, and it is the highest elevation in Arizona.

The road going south from Cameron presently begins to mount the steady slope of the thickening lava bed. The air grows somewhat cooler, the vegetation is more profuse and represents a different community. For the moment we are retracing in an opposite direction the stages we passed through when we descended from the rim to the desert around Cameron. Cactus now gives way to the piñon pine characteristic of the rim and then, as we mount higher, to the ponderosa which dominates the high north rim. A few miles north of Flagstaff one must turn west onto an unsurfaced mountain road leading toward a pass over which it mounts steeply, up and up. Presently it ends at a ski bowl above which the ultimate summit towers darkly. We are in a forest of pines and firs which "indicate" the Hudsonian zone and we have thus passed through five of the life zones of the Northern Hemisphere. The air is chilly, but in very early October there is no snow yet, though there might have been and soon will be. Obviously there has been hard frost just above, since the great patches of aspen which break the mantle of evergreen are dazzlingly colored in the clear sunshine. Looking almost vertically upward one can see the tree line and above it the Arctic meadows.

It would be a long hard climb to reach them from this side, but one may at least look into the Arctic zone and realize that one has seen, within a few hours, the whole range of vegetational communities of North America except for the truly Tropical. Nowhere in the East and only at a few places in the West can one journey so far in so short a time. When Thoreau said that he had traveled extensively in Concord, that was a paradox. To say it of Coconino County is to make a simple statement of fact.

That evening my mind went back to the brilliant patches of aspen which here and there, for no apparent reason, seemed to be successfully disputing the mountain slopes with the more prevalent evergreens, and I wondered why. Some people think it is better to leave such questions alone and to take the beauty of nature for granted. If sufficiently phlegmatic they may take the attitude of the legendary English visitor who refused to see anything wonderful about all the water which tumbles over Niagara because, as he asked, "What's to prevent it?" Some of the more philosophically inclined may, like Wordsworth, object to what he called "peeping and botanizing." But there are others—and I am among them—who find themselves seeing it more vividly when nature is not merely a spectacle but a phenomenon interpretable in terms of the infinitely complex and subtle processes of which the spectacle is an outward and visible sign. And I have never found either the beauty or the wonder diminished.

Why then the colorful aspens? In this region the evergreens represent the climax vegetation. They are in stable equilibrium with themselves and their environment. They may tolerate a few aspens here and there but they would

Thus far shalt thou go

never, if left undisturbed, permit them to take over as they so obviously have done in the large brilliant patches. It is not, be it understood, that evergreens are always in other parts of the world a climax. Throughout many places in the East the situation is reversed. Pines are the first trees to take over a cleared spot and then, three-quarters of a century later, they are being ousted by the deciduous trees whose seedlings grew up in the shade they provided, and these deciduous trees establish the stable equilibrium which will last until something violent disturbs it. But here it is the evergreens that are ultimately dominant.

The first part of the answer to the question, "Why large patches of aspen in a climax forest of pines?" is "fire." A bolt of lightning or perhaps a camper's match burns a patch an acre or many acres in size. Then the wind or some animal agency brings in the aspen seeds which have been produced in vast numbers just waiting for such an opportunity and are light enough to blow. Not only do they seize their chance quickly, but they have several advantages over the pine. For one thing, the seedlings can stand the heat of an unbroken flood of sunlight; for another, they can take root in the ash to which the humus covering of the lava has been reduced; for a third, they grow very quickly. And for all these reasons they can take over before the pines can re-occupy the land.

But they are not, for all that, a permanent or climax growth. They are quite short-lived. Within a century or even less they are growing old. They are also killing one another off by their own shade. Meanwhile, however, they have added new humus to the soil and they have provided shade fatal to them but not to pine seedlings. By the time they die or are crowded out, the evergreens are already occupying their former plot of ground. Thus in Arizona aspen stands are nearly always mere stopgaps, and within a few generations the climax has been reached again, though meanwhile fire has probably prepared elsewhere the way for another patch of aspen to gladden the traveler's eye. Nor is the human traveler the only creature who profits from them. Many animals from rabbits to porcupines, beavers, deer and, northward, even the moose are to some extent dependent upon the aspen's buds or bark. In many places the animal community would not be what it is, were it not for the accidents which permit the stability of the climax condition to be, from time to time, broken.

To know this does not diminish my purely aesthetic pleasure in the splashes of gold against the dark green of the mountain side. They are perhaps no more beautiful; but they are more interesting. And they are also something more than an occasion for an isolated piece of information. As another evidence of the intricate wholeness of the natural world, they are what I would call "an aid to contemplation."

8

The paradox of a lava flow

Those tourists who turn off the main highway just south of Cameron and head for the south rim sometimes see, just at the junction, a shocking sight. Perched atop the stone marker is a little Navajo boy wearing a brightly colored feather headdress of the sort one buys at the five-and-dime. He is hoping you will give him a dollar to pose for a picture.

Whatever else the Navajos—and they are relatively recent invaders of the Southwest—may or may not have learned from the white man, there is one thing they have learned: You must give the tourist what he wants, and what he wants is what he expects, rather than what is true or authentic. No Indian who ever lived within hundreds of miles of the Canyon ever wore anything remotely resembling this head-dress, which is a cheap parody of what the Indians of the plains far to the east did wear. But an Indian is supposed to live in a tepee and to sport a trailing circlet of feathers. And it is a picture of what an Indian is popularly supposed to look like that too many tourists want to take home.

Actually, of course, Arizona, Colorado and New Mexico were inhabited for centuries before the white man came by various Indian peoples whose indigenous culture had reached a high level. The seven Golden Cities of which Coronado had heard rumors never existed except in the imagination of his Mexican informants—who may or may not have believed their own tales. But cities there were, teeming with clever craftsmen and builders who practiced a scientific agriculture and developed domestic arts to a very high degree. In fact, with the possible exception of the Iroquois, no other aboriginal inhabitants north of what is now the Mexican border ever achieved so high a degree of civilization. It had already declined disastrously before the white man came, but scattered over three states are imposing remains of the cities built while the plains Indians were living in mud huts.

Wild West shows and children's books have made it inevitable that "aborigines" should bring first to mind a picture of the red man on horseback pursuing a buffalo. But

The paradox of a lava flow

Indians had no horses before the white man came, and neither on the plains nor anywhere else was he leading that life in pre-Spanish days. The whole plains Indian culture is a post-white-contact phenomenon.

Like all the aboriginal inhabitants of the New World, the southwestern Indians had come, pretty certainly, from Asia and across at the point where the two continents once either joined or were at least nearer to contact than they are now. But to the question "when?" rapidly changing answers have been given. A generation ago there was no evidence that Indians had been here for more than five thousand years, and it was sometimes categorically stated that they had not. But new discoveries have pushed the date back and back. Spearheads have been found associated with the bones of mammoths which Indian hunters killed. There were red men in the Southwest fifteen or twenty or perhaps even more thousands of years ago, and that, incidentally, means for approximately as long as the ancestors of the modern European are known to have been in Europe.

Between then and the beginning of the historical period various cultures rose and fell. The bow and arrow supplanted the throwing stick. Agriculture supplemented hunting as the essential occupation. Underground pit houses were replaced by structures of stone or dobe, basket making and then pottery became essential domestic arts. The relation between the various cultures is by no means always clear. There are roundhead and longhead types. What part was played by conquest, what by peaceful absorption is also not always certain. But there was a long rise in the development of civilization which reached its climax toward the end of the thirteenth century when the great communal dwellings, whose remains are still scattered over a wide area and are sometimes in a remarkable state of preservation, were completed.

Then, within the span of a few years, they were abandoned for reasons still under investigation. A disastrous twenty-year drought probably played an important role but so, possibly, did warfare with newcomers into the region. The people found here by the first white men did not themselves know what their relation to the vanished, more prosperous people had been.

South America as well as what is now Mexico had presumably been populated by groups which moved farther and farther southward. But why the Mayas and others achieved a complex intellectual civilization very far in advance of even the most successful of the inhabitants of our Southwest is a still unanswered question, and one hotly disputed theory maintains that their rapid development can be explained only on the assumption that contact had been made across the South Pacific with the more highly developed people of the East.

At various times important centers of a flourishing communal life lay north, south, east and west of the Canyon which, even twenty thousand years ago must have been much like what it is today. But neither in its depth nor on its rims is there any evidence that it was ever more than sparsely inhabited.

It is true that the earliest white visitors found small Indian groups, one of which was living where the only surviving members of the tribe still live, namely some sixty miles west of the tourist center and about two thousand feet below the rim. Theirs is a warm, cozy little side canyon watered by Cataract Creek which tumbles in falls and gathers in clear pools. Though the area is now technically a communally owned reservation with a government school and some help from an agricultural agent, the life of this tribe is in many ways still what it was two hundred years ago. Its members raise beans and squash and they still know how to roast the great flower bud of the agave ("century plant") in pits heated by hot stones. Now they also cultivate peaches and graze a few cattle. Formerly, at least, they supplemented the more conventional foods with cactus fruit and the bulbs of the sago lily which, so it is said, tastes much like sweet potato. Havasupai, the name by which they know themselves, means "People of the Blue-green Water" in reference to the turquoise color of the mineral-laden water when it collects into pools.

Their language links them with the Yuman group to the southwest, but for long their early history was largely a matter of guesswork. A few years ago Douglas Schwartz, then a graduate student at Yale University, undertook extensive investigations on the spot and seems to have established the general outlines. Their immediate ancestors, a now vanished people, known as the Cohonia, seem to have occupied the plateau country south of the Canyon as long ago as 600 A.D. They flourished greatly, and when all the accustomed land was occupied, some of them discovered the well-watered Canyon below the rim. There they invented or borrowed the technique of irrigation for the cultivation of summer crops but moved up to the plateau in winter. Then when hostile tribes invaded the original homeland of the Cohonia, more of them were driven into the Canyon and there they were probably joined by refugees from other tribes who helped develop a distinctive Canyon culture.

It had obviously been long established when in 1776 the Franciscan Father Garces set down in his diary the earliest written notice of their existence. Head of the Spanish mission at Tucson, he had set out without any white companions on an extended journey which took him not only to Cataract Canyon, but ultimately across the Little Colorado somewhere near the modern town of Cameron and on to the Hopi villages to the east. It was June when, after an arduous trip, he reached the Havasupai, and isolated though their position seemed to make them, they nevertheless obviously carried on an active trade with other tribes who were in contact with the whites. In his diary Father Garces wrote: "I had much complacency to see that as soon as it was dawn each married man with his wife went forth to till his *milpas,* taking the necessary implements, as hatchet, dibble and hoe, all of which they procure from the Moqui [i.e., Hopi]. These people go decently clothed and are very fond of a

red cloth of Castillia which comes from New Mexico.* That
the women here are so white—I saw one who looked like an
Española—I attribute to the situation of the place which
they have; for this is so deep that it is ten o'clock when the
sun begins to shine. Whithersoever I have gone I have seen
no situation more strong and secure by nature."

Though Father Garces called the settlement the largest
he had seen so far in the region, he added that "these families do not exceed thirty-four in number." Apparently the
population has been extraordinarily stable. In 1858, Lieutenant Ives estimated it at about two hundred, and in 1881
Elliot Couès reported 214. A recent census of families again
counted thirty-four, or precisely the number which composed the community in 1776. No other Indians now live
within the park area—unless you count the Hopi employees
of the Harvey hotels, some of whom live in their own quarters at the tourist center.

At no time during the centuries before the white man
came does there appear to have been any large human
population at or in the Canyon. To be sure some five hundred ruins have been found within what is now the national
park area, but they are mostly very small affairs and they
represent a long stretch of time. A few of the remains go
back to the beginning of the Christian era, and one of the
largest seems to have been abandoned about 900 A.D. An-

---

* This "red cloth" was that used for the uniforms of the Spanish soldiers
and was often unraveled by the Indians who re-wove the thread into their
own fabrics, some specimens of which re-weaving survive as important
collector's items.

other, whose excavated ground plan is exposed near the archeological museum on the south rim was built near the end of the twelfth century, included a two-story living section, a series of one-story storage rooms entered by ladders leading to hatchways in the roof, and an enclosed courtyard in the center. Some twenty-five or thirty people probably inhabited this structure but only for a short time. The rubbish heap is small, and there are no burials. Probably the center was inhabited for a mere twenty-five years or so before it was abandoned at about the same time as the other pueblos in the immediate region. It is believed that the inhabitants first moved northeast and then took part in a general exodus southward when the great drought struck. There is evidence that at much later dates Hopis and even Navajos paid at least visits to the Canyon. But it must always have been more or less on the fringe of the densely occupied areas. There were better places to live.

One of these better places lay just a little to the southeast in the area dominated by the huge cinder cone we noticed in passing on our way from the Canyon to the alpine peaks of the San Francisco Mountains. For a century or two the region round about was occupied by a flourishing, fast-growing community which presently vanished. But it was not, as you might well imagine, destroyed by the great volcanic eruption which covered hundreds of square miles with lava. Instead, it was created by that same lava flow, and

The paradox of a lava flow

thereby hangs one of the strangest tales of southwestern archeology.

We know that nations have often risen and fallen as their soil increased or diminished in fertility. This is usually a slow and often obscure process. But here on a small stage and within a very brief span of years a striking drama was played out. Its theme was the ultimate dependence of "prosperity" upon the soil at a peoples' disposal. And the eruption had temporarily improved that soil.

The story begins at the very end of a recent epoch of intense volcanic activity whose mightiest effort resulted in the building of the San Francisco Peaks now nearly thirteen thousand feet above sea level, five thousand above the plateau on which they rest, and once were at least three thousand higher still. These cones must have been built rather recently. They rest upon the same Kaibab limestone which forms the rim of the Canyon and that means that the overlying strata must, as at the Canyon, have been eroded away before the volcanoes burst forth. Still, the most violent activity certainly occurred before there were any men to witness or be destroyed by it. But the activity subsided gradually over a long period, and minor outbreaks occurred from time to time. There are at least two hundred cinder cones built up later than the San Francisco Peaks, and the most recent of all (as well as the most spectacular) is Sunset Crater. When it was created man was already long established nearby.

GRAND CANYON

Visible from the highway a few miles north of Flagstaff the stark cone is likely to catch the eye of the least observant tourist, because it is so obviously what he has imagined a volcano to be. The symmetrical cone, truncated at the top, rises steeply like a gigantic anthill, its sides the grayish-black of cinder and almost completely bare of vegetation. Plainly, nature has not had time to reconquer it as she has reconquered the San Francisco Peaks. It is an unhealed scar, grimly beautiful but also a mute reminder of a catastrophe which looks as though it might have struck a few years instead of a few centuries ago.

Turn off onto the graded road which leads east a few miles to the base of the cone, and the sense that one is in the presence of a recent yesterday grows stronger and stronger. Those who come, as we do, from the Canyon to the north have been for many miles accustomed to stretches of black desert whose surface is partly covered with lava. But here the road is traversing a bed of clinkerlike fragments so jagged and tumbled that it is difficult to walk over them. It is a desolate nightmarishly beautiful scene of unearthly desolation, and of desolation which looks so newly wrecked that one almost expects to see the lava still smoking. Suddenly the road, which has been climbing a rather steep slope, stops at the base of the abruptly rising cone. From there it is a slow, hot climb, a mile long and a thousand feet up, to the crater itself. The rim is stained an angry red responsible for its name. In the distance to the east shimmers the Painted Desert. Looking down into the crater, one half-expects to see a lake of still boiling lava.

That the catastrophe was not really as recent as one feels it might have been is proved by the few trees which have managed to establish themselves here and there around the cone's base and sometimes look as though they had just been half-buried in the cinders. Actually, the eruption (as unusually good evidence proves) took place a little less than a thousand years ago.

By comparison with the earlier eruptions in the same general area, that of Sunset Crater was a rather small affair. Still, it piled up a cone that is even today a thousand feet high, and covered with basaltic sand an area of some eight hundred square miles to a depth which still ranges from more than a foot near the cone to a fraction of an inch at the periphery. Naturally, all the vegetation must have been killed over most of this area. And the burned-out remains of Indian dwellings plainly overwhelmed by the catastrophe have been excavated.

But when the sand and cinder cooled, a surprising phenomenon occurred: the land became temporarily more fertile than before—not because the sand and cinder provided any nourishment, but because they acted as a mulch. In desert regions anything that retards the evaporation of the scanty rainfall promotes the growth of plants. One may see the effect today near the base of the cone where vegetation flourishes only where one would, at first thought, suppose it to be impossible—namely, on, or rather under, the foot or more drifts of cinder. Nothing, one would have said, could grow there. But plants, rooted in the soil beneath, have pushed their way up through the cinders to bear flowers and fruit, whereas a few feet away the ground is parched and dead.

Present-day desert dwellers notice the same phenomenon when weeds and wildflowers, elsewhere absent, come up in the gravel-covered areas of their patios. And on a grander scale the same phenomenon is exhibited on the slopes of the San Francisco Peaks. The summits and the summits only of the mountains round about are crowned with juniper and pine because only at higher elevations is there enough rainfall to support them. But the better a given area is mulched with cinder, the less rainfall is necessary, and the forests follow the cinders downward. Northward and southward the lower limit of pine follows the seven-thousand-foot contour line. Where the cinder covering is deep, the lower limit drops a thousand feet. Moreover, the growth rings of the cinder-mulched trees are wide, thus indicating abundant moisture.

The Hopi Indians who now live on mesa tops some miles to the east and grow corn on the sandy desert still take advantage of the phenomenon. They dig a hole in the sand, sometimes as much as eighteen inches deep, and at the bottom of it they plant their seed corn. Any farmer of a kindlier land would tell them it would never come up. But it does. Rooted in the moist soil beneath the sand it pushes through,

The paradox of a lava flow

and though never very high above the surface, it ripens the grain which supports the tribe and has done so for so many hundreds of years that one of the Hopi villages is known to have been continuously inhabited for a longer time than (so far as is known) any other community within the United States. Lines of heavy stones placed at strategic spots anchor the sand and prevent it from blowing away or piling into drifts. Some Indian community—composed possibly of the Hopis' ancestors—understood the value of a cinder mulch shortly after the time of the Sunset eruption, and they took advantage of it.

About 1916 Dr. Harold S. Colton of the Museum of Northern Arizona at Flagstaff began an archeological survey of the region which has continued ever since. A certain relatively small number of the ancient dwellings lay beneath the cinder layer, and their charred timbers testified to a fiery destruction. Artifacts (especially pottery) found in both the buried sites and in some of the dwellings built on top of the cinder covering revealed that both had been inhabited during that stage of culture sometimes known as Pueblo II which originated about 700 A.D. and flourished for several hundred years until it was succeeded by that of the great cliff dwellings like Mesa Verde in Colorado. But Professor A. E. Douglass' recently developed tree-ring scale made it possible to be much more precise than that. Given a good specimen of timber, it is possible to determine, within a few years, the date at which it was cut; and by using various samples, including what seemed to be the most recent, Professor Douglass concluded that the eruption must have occurred between 875 and 1276. Subsequent further investigation, including coordination of the tree-ring data with the evidence of the then rapidly changing pottery styles, has led Dr. Colton to narrow the gap and to place it as after 1046 and before 1071. In other words, this Indian community was destroyed about the time William the Conqueror set sail for England.

But the most striking paradox is that which the secret of the mulching effect of volcanic sand and cinder enables us to understand. Dwellings built on top of the cinders (and hence subsequent to the eruption) are far more numerous than those prior to it. The catastrophe was a blessing also, even if very much disguised. The people who moved back into the area after it had cooled prospered greatly. Their dwellings can be dated and for perhaps two hundred years they enjoyed the benefits of unusually fertile land. Then the prevailing west winds piled the volcanic sand into drifts too deep for cultivation while it laid surrounding areas bare. That the inhabitants knew what was happening is evident from the lines of stone, still visible, which anxious cultivators had laid down in an effort to anchor the mulch. But it was a losing battle, and after 1300 the area was abandoned.

What happened to the vanished population? Did it simply die out as conditions became impossibly hard, or did survivors move elsewhere? There are no certain facts which will answer that question. But where archeology stops, an-

The paradox of a lava flow

thropology supplies a basis for fascinating and not unreasonable speculation.

Those Hopis who were already in Coronado's time living on their still rather inaccessible mesas to the west are an unusual and interesting people. They are serene, conservative and peaceful, though so fiercely independent that in 1680 they expelled the Spaniards after killing their missionaries. And unlike some of the other pueblo dwelling peoples, they have never as a group either accepted Christianity or much changed their way of life. They still farm by the ancient method, make pottery, and practice the elaborate religious rites which are an important part of a close communal life. Their gods are the grotesque but mostly benign Kachinas, and for the education as well as the amusement of their children they make those Kachina dolls of which cheap imitations are widely sold in curio shops throughout the Southwest. But an odd feature of their religion is this: the home of the gods is not in the region nearby but on the San Francisco Peaks which dominate the landscape near the now deserted area around Sunset Crater, and the Hopis still make pilgrimages to the peaks for religious reasons.

Notoriously, religion is the most conservative part of most cultures. We ourselves still tend to build our churches in an ancient architectural style. Similarly many pueblo dwelling groups conduct their religious ceremonies in "kivas" which appear to be modeled on the ancient pit houses which were the usual kind of dwelling house before the above-ground pueblos were developed. Does the fact that the Hopis' sacred mountain is so far away from their present home suggest that they once lived near that sacred mountain? Did they migrate from the once favorable but now no longer cultivatable area of the Sunset Crater lava field, taking their religion and their agriculture with them but leaving their gods where they had always been?

Among the Hopi legends there is, in any event, one that tells of a destruction of the wicked by fire. In a certain village, so the legend runs, a good chief was disturbed by the degeneracy of his people—especially by the fact that even the women would join in the gambling games to which the whole tribe was disastrously addicted. One night he noticed light in the mountains. He told his people about it, but they ridiculed him and went on with their games. During four successive nights the light grew brighter and the fire began to spread out toward the village. But the gamblers refused to heed the warning and ridiculed the chief whom they accused of trying to frighten them away from their games. Finally, too late for most, they realized the danger and were either suffocated or burned to death. Only a few who had fled in time were saved.

This seems pretty clearly a memory of some volcanic eruption, though there is no evidence of any recent one near where the Hopis now live. Perhaps—but of course only perhaps—it goes back to Sunset Crater and the flight of the original inhabitants some of whose descendants later re-

The paradox of a lava flow

turned only to abandon the region again when the wind had made it infertile once more.

The eruption of Sunset Crater was, then, only a minor catastrophe and only a short-lived blessing—hardly important enough to be mentioned among the innumerable ups and downs which constitute the history of man on this earth. Similarly, to have pin-pointed it in time is only a minor triumph of the various new techniques for establishing chronology. But these techniques make possible many other interesting tales.

Even a generation ago geologists and archeologists alike could deduce only vague dates. Now the margin of error in archeology has been reduced from centuries to decades, and in relatively recent geology from hundreds of thousands of years to thousands or even hundreds. The amount of radioactive carbon 14 remaining in any preserved fragment of organic matter formed within the last 25,000 years will reveal pretty accurately how long ago it ceased to live and grow. The tree-ring pattern in a surviving piece of timber will, in the Southwest at least, tell when it started to grow and when it died.

More simply—and as has long been known—merely to count the annual rings in a recently cut tree is to learn how old it is. And this simple technique has revealed a startling fact: The longest lived organism now on earth is not, as was supposed until recently, the giant redwood, but a gnarled and battered little pine some specimens of which grow high up on the San Francisco Peaks. And thus in the Canyon country one may see not only some of the oldest known rocks but also the most long enduring species of living things. In rocks "old" means a billion or more years; in living things four or five thousand. Every traveler has noticed the brilliant aspens and the towering ponderosa pines. But no one, not even foresters and other professional students of trees, ever paid much attention to the bristlecone pine until, just a year or two ago, the astonishing age of some specimens was discovered.

As a recognized species it had been known to science for more than a hundred years. F. Creutzfeldt, botanist accompanying the Pacific Railway survey in 1853, noticed it growing on the mountains of Colorado and collected a bough two months before he was murdered by Indians in the famous and bloody Gunnison Massacre. Botany was not in those days a very safe science, and David Douglas, for whom the Douglas fir is named, lost his life in the course of his plant exploration when he was trampled by a wild bull. But there were stay-at-home botanists to classify what the adventurers found, and the bristlecone was baptized with a Latin name: *Pinus aristata.*

There for a long time the matter rested. Growing as it does high in the mountains of California, Colorado, Arizona and other western states from an altitude of 7,500 feet to the extreme limit of tree growth at more than twelve thousand, it has no value as timber and is not, like the Douglas fir, a possible ornament. Only the scientific and the imaginative were likely to be attracted by a tree whose chief distinction seemed to be its extraordinary tenacity in keeping alive where no other tree could. Under very favorable conditions it may grow to forty or fifty feet, but where it clings to a few handfuls of soil in some rock crevice of a wind-swept summit it is dwarfed, twisted, broken—seemingly just alive in one or two limbs struggling out of a trunk from which most of the bark and living tissue has been stripped away. What you would never guess is that, far from being moribund, it may have been living in much the same state for thousands of years and be quite prepared to live hundreds (possibly thousands) more.

Obviously, its growth must be extraordinarily slow where the soil is so poor, where snow may fall in nearly every month of the year, and the average temperature be only a degree or two above freezing. In fact, it had been known for some time that a specimen six or seven feet high might show nearly a thousand annual rings. But it remained for Professor Edmund Schulman, of the Laboratory of Tree-ring Research at the University of Arizona, to follow a lead suggested by his observation that the oldest known trees seemed to be those which had grown slowly. Because few if any other trees have grown so slowly as some of the most unfavorably situated bristlecones, might they, he asked himself, be the very oldest also?

Using the specially designed borer which removes a cylindrical plug without seriously damaging a tree, Professor

GRAND CANYON

Schulman investigated some unusually stunted and twisted specimens in the White Mountains of eastern California. One whose rings have been counted turns out to be more than four thousand years old—which makes it nearly a thousand years older than the oldest definitely dated redwood. This would mean that it was already a thousand years old when the Trojan War was fought and that the seed must have sprouted at a time when the birth of Christ was as far in the future as it is now in the past.

From photographs you might suppose that it was by now on its last legs. Much of the bark has retreated, the central trunk has been broken off, and the remaining small limbs seem to have been tortured by the winds. Yet though Professor Schulman will not guess how much longer it may live, he does say that, despite its appearance, it seems to be in excellent health. A polished section of another very ancient specimen which I have had the privilege of examining is a beautiful light yellow in color and so fine-grained that it seems almost to have no grain at all. Only the microscope reveals, in a state of perfect preservation, the narrow growth rings and the delicate cellular structure formed several thousand years ago. No bristlecone from the San Francisco Peaks is known to be so old as those from California. In fact, the oldest so far examined has been growing for a mere millennium and a half. Even so it must have been five hundred years old when fire burst out of the ground where Sunset Crater now stands and the human inhabitants fled elsewhere.

The paradox of a lava flow

In spring the desert flats round about are sprinkled with gay little annuals which must mature so rapidly during the brief time when there is a little moisture in the soil that some of them rush from seed to seed again in a mere six weeks. They are among the most short-lived of plant organisms and they grow within sight of the most enduring.

All living things—at least, all above the level of the one-celled protozoa—must die. Moreover, for each one there seems to be a natural life span which may not be greatly exceeded. But what sets the limit and why it should vary so enormously from species to species is a mystery upon which very little light has ever been thrown. Why, even if given the most favorable possible conditions, should death ineluctably overtake some plants after a few brief weeks while the bristlecone and the redwood may live for thousands of years? Why can no man live much more than a hundred years and why (despite legends and tall tales) does it appear that no backboned animal can exceed that time by more than about 50 per cent? A worker bee born in the summer season reaches the end of her rope in about six weeks; a house mouse at two years will almost inevitably fall a victim to senile cancer. Has it all something to do, not merely with a span of time, but with the completion of some cycle of development? The fact that the slowest growing trees of the bristlecone species live longest suggests that the more rapidly a certain potentiality is used up, the sooner it is irreparably exhausted.

GRAND CANYON

Nobody knows why. Perhaps, however, someone will find out. And conceivably—just barely conceivably—the knowledge may make it possible for men to live longer.

The fact remains, nevertheless, that increasing his allotted life span is precisely the thing that man, despite all his triumphs over disease, has not been able to do. The average length of life has been greatly increased. Because "unnatural" death is so often prevented, more men than ever before reach to something like their normal allotment of years. But nothing suggests that the oldest are any older than they were when civilization began. Whether or not men really want to live longer is another question. Most do not now act as though they did.

9

The longest ten miles

When most visitors, most map makers and even the post office say "Grand Canyon," they mean the south rim. It is the more accessible from the great centers of population and, because the river keeps closer, perhaps the best place to get a quick grasp of the mighty reality. Far more tourists stop there and it is, for the most part, what we have been describing. But across the awful gulf there is, of course, another precipitous edge.

It has its hotel, campgrounds and other facilities almost directly opposite the south rim village. The two are just ten miles apart and from either side one may see at night what looks like a single twinkling light not so very far away. Only the least curious can help wondering what is "over there" and how one may get to it. To most, the answer to the first of these questions is more encouraging than the answer to the second. What is over there is, in fact, a very different world.

The difference is not a geological one. The traveler who makes the trip will find himself again on the great dome of rock through which the river cut as the dome rose under it. The exposed surface is again that Kaibab limestone laid down under a shallow sea something like 200,000,000 years ago. The successive strata exposed as the river cut deeper and deeper are perfectly matched, one side with another. Underneath the Kaibab comes the desert-deposited Coconino, below that the red shale, then the Mississippian Redwall, and so on down to the inconceivably old black rocks at the bottom of the inner gorge.

But the north rim lies higher up the slope of the dome—rather more than a thousand feet higher—and that makes all the difference. At its highest point it is 8801 feet above sea level—which means cooler summers and cold, cold winters. Still more importantly it means more rainfall; and in country predominantly arid, rainfall is the most important factor. The average annual precipitation at the south rim is approximately fourteen inches, at the north rather more than twenty-three. Also, far more of it comes down as snow whose

The longest ten miles

slow melting gives deep penetration to the roots of great forest trees.

During February, the coldest month, the average minimum temperature is nine above zero, and the average annual snowfall is more than twelve and a half feet. No wonder that the access roads are closed from the middle of October until late spring and the whole area deserted except for two snowbound caretakers who stay behind, completely isolated for months, and busy chiefly in keeping the snow from crushing the roofs of the buildings. But from June to October one is aware only of a delightful coolness and of the blessings a relatively abundant precipitation brings. At the south rim the dominant tree is the scrawny if picturesque piñon pine. On the north rim a great forest of fir, spruce, ponderosa pine and aspen stretches northward, frequently and delightfully relieved by large alpine meadows gay with flowers.

How shall one get to this so different but almost contiguous world? Certain squirrels and various other creatures have, as the reader may remember, never made it. For them the rim of the Canyon is the rim of the world. Ravens and some other large birds sail casually across but, as the bird-banders have discovered, the small songsters do not like a mile of abyss below them, and when they cross, they proceed cautiously down one side and up the other much as the earth-bound mules make the trip.

Unless one has the wings of a bird—and of a large bird at

GRAND CANYON

that—only two courses are open. The shortest, but by no means the quickest way, is the very strenuous two-day journey on muleback a vertical mile down to the river and almost a mile and a quarter up again. In less than half that time, in five or six hours to be exact, you may drive an automobile down off the dome, north along the river, across the only bridge spanning the Colorado for many hundred miles, up the dome again, and then southward to the Canyon rim just ten airline miles from the point at which you started. The distance is 215 miles, and that makes the ten the raven flies one of the longest in the world.

Tourists in a hurry—as tourists usually are—not infrequently complain that "they" ought to do something about this absurdly long round about. They talk vaguely of a possible cable car down one side and up the other and sometimes express indignation when they learn that the public all-weather air strips are, respectively, twenty miles south of the south rim and eighty miles north of the north rim. Someday, I regret to say, progress may gratify their desire to see as little as possible as quickly as possible. Then they will be able to miss one of the most impressive reminders of what a stupendous discontinuity the ages have established and also the whole of the 215-mile drive—which is one of the most varied and magnificent in a region of varied and magnificent journeys. I have made it many times and I have yet to wish that a cable car could take me across the abyss instead.

The road runs eastward and downward past the junction

The longest ten miles

of the Colorado and the Little Colorado until it reaches the desert flat; then northward for more than seventy miles across that desert; then westward up the dome of the Kaibab Plateau again; then southward through the forests to the rim. From the road one sees, sometimes close at hand, sometimes far away, the mountains, cliffs and buttes formed of sedimentary rocks laid down millions of years later than the surface he is traveling on.

Layers of those same formations once covered the whole area. But because it had been lifted to a steeper angle, they had all been eroded away, probably before the cutting of the Canyon even began. And though these later formations are much of the time in sight, the road itself rarely traverses anything except the Kaibab sandstone. Here, as on the two contrasting rims, the variety is not one created by a difference in the geological age of the formations but almost exclusively the result of altitude, of slope, and of rainfall. Sparse desert and dense forest rest upon the same floor.

The first fifty-odd miles are over the same road we followed down off the dome on our visit to Sunset Crater. Then, just at the bottom of the declivity where the little crossroads center of Cameron shimmers on the desert, we turn north instead of south, putting the San Francisco peaks at our back. A narrow suspension bridge carries us across the Little Colorado (sometimes quite dry but a swift stream after a wet summer as when I last passed over it), and the road lies straight ahead through that unusually bare desert which is the Navajo Indian reservation. It stretches to the Utah border on the north and into New Mexico and the Colorado border on the east, covering some 25,000 square miles or about one-fifth of the total area of Arizona. Nevertheless, the allotment is not so generous as it sounds. Strange and fascinating as the whole area is to look at, a land less hospitable to a human being who tries to live in it is hard to imagine. Most of the red sandy surface is bare of all vegetation and only dotted here and there by little clumps of straggling, struggling vegetation.

Yet people do live here and extract from the hopeless-looking terrain some sort of sustenance. In fact, the Navajo tribe has increased greatly and it must be admitted that, unproductive as the land was when they were compelled to settle upon it, overgrazing—partly by too many horses kept primarily for show—has made it even more barren. Keep your eyes peeled and you will see, often only a few hundred feet from the road but so devoid of contrast as to be hardly visible, one of the cylindrical log-and-wood hogans in which the Navajos live during the high cold winter and, probably, a brush shelter for summer beside it. Less often you will see one of the Indians themselves on horseback or perhaps be compelled to stop while a flock of sheep (always accompanied by a few goats to supply intelligent leadership) crosses the road. In charge will be a Navajo woman or a tiny Navajo girl, either the one or the other dressed in the velvet blouse and voluminous skirts adopted long ago from the Spanish invaders and stubbornly adhered to for centuries, despite the fact that the skirts, especially, seem perversely

The longest ten miles

ill-suited to either the occupations or the summer heat. The men are rather more sensibly dressed but they don't, by tradition, herd sheep.

In good years you may also see, in especially favorable spots, a few deep-planted fields of corn. But the sheep which manage somehow to sustain life on the sparse vegetation are the Navajos' chief livelihood. From their wool they spin thread and then weave the blankets and rugs which, together with sacks of wool, they sell to the traders for food. You must wait patiently while the flock, often in no great hurry, crosses the road. After all, the land is theirs and their masters'. You may wave a greeting if you like, but the chances are that it will not be acknowledged. And you had better not try to take a photograph. Little boys near Cameron may put on a headdress and be glad to pose—for a consideration. Reservation dwellers are likely to consider photography an impudent invasion of their privacy. And they have not all forgot that it was the white man who starved them out of the canyons where they had taken refuge and thus brought them to ignominious surrender and the necessity of confining themselves to this cruel land.

Except for the Hopis to the east, few Indian tribes have stuck more stubbornly to their way of life. And yet, as it is strange to remember, that way is largely a borrowed, not an aboriginal one. Until the Spaniards came they wore no velvet jackets, owned no sheep or horses and were ignorant of both the art of weaving wool and the art of working silver, though today it is a very poor Navajo indeed who does not

GRAND CANYON

sport a considerable weight of the silver buttons, belts, and other ornaments he or one of his fellows has fashioned. The way of life is theirs now, and they could not be more loyal to it were its traditions as old as the tribe itself.

How much longer it will or can last is, however, a question. Twenty years ago when I first met them, a few had acquired model T Fords, and I still remember the bewildering incongruity of a family arriving at a remote trader's post chauffeured by a pater familias who knew how to drive a jalopy but had hung a blanket between the front and back seats because he still believed that if he so much as caught sight of his mother-in-law he would go blind. The discovery of uranium on the reservation is likely to make more and faster changes as the Indians are given compensation for the invasion of their territory. Already I have seen parked in front of a mud hogan, not a jalopy, but a car far newer and shinier than my own.

For something less than a hundred miles the road runs due north over almost level ground, although, just a little to the right of it, red sandstone cliffs rise higher and higher. Then suddenly one reaches the Colorado as it comes in from the northeast between the high rock walls of Marble Canyon. Here a suspension bridge 834 feet long and nearly five hundred feet above the river was built in 1929, the only bridge (except for the one we crossed on muleback at the bottom of the Canyon) between Moab, Utah, and Lake Mead, or for a distance of about a thousand miles. You turn sharp westward just before crossing, and with the great Vermilion Cliffs on your right, you run along their base for another twenty-odd miles before the road starts to wind upward again to reach the top of the dome through which the river cut its way.

Most travelers cross the bridge in a hurry, glancing briefly if at all at the river below and, almost before they know it, they have crossed what was for many years a formidable barrier to travel. Good roads are fine and I am glad of the bridge. But it is a pity to stick so slavishly to the pavement as not to realize how close one is in this country to a primitive world cut by a narrow ribbon of modernization which scarcely affects what lies even a few hundred yards to either side.

Few notice (and fewer follow) a primitive dirt road taking off just beyond the bridge and leading back toward the river. If you follow it for five miles across red desert strewn with broken sandstone hillocks, you are very unlikely to meet any other traveler, though a dozen or more cars will probably have crossed the bridge and gone on while you were exploring. Presently you will come to a spot where the riverbank is low on your side, a precipitous cliff on the other. Slanting down the side of the cliff a sort of ramp cut into the rock is still visible and obviously intended to make it possible for men and wagons to descend from the cliff top to the river.

This is the site of Lee's Ferry. For many years it was the only crossing of the Colorado in 270 miles. It is also associated with an odd and bloody series of events which seem very remote, though the drama was played out less than a hundred years ago. John D. Lee, a renegade Mormon leader, was living there with his family in 1877 when soldiers of the United States took him in charge and conducted him to Mountain Meadows, Utah, where he was executed for a crime committed twenty years before and one which, according to Lee, had been no crime at all—though by his own admission he had been one of the leaders of a group which had massacred a party of 115 (some say 123) men and women immigrants from Arkansas and Mississippi.

In the East, it must be remembered, the Mormons had themselves been the victims of a massacre committed by "gentiles" who were the unprovoked aggressors. The Mormons had then accomplished a heroic trek to Utah and, conquering seemingly impossible obstacles, they had established a flourishing community well beyond the frontier in a region where they hoped to live in peace by their peculiar convictions. It is no wonder that they saw with alarm the vanguards of a civilization they had reason to fear penetrating a world they had occupied for themselves. Massacres of whites by Indians and of Indians by whites were familiar occurrences. They were drastic but not universally disapproved methods of dealing with enemy peoples who penetrated what the inhabitants regarded as their territory. Example is a powerful teacher—especially if you have first been the victims, not the perpetrators.

The longest ten miles

Exactly what happened at Mountain Meadows is still a matter of dispute. According to one story, the original attackers were Indians; according to another they were Mormon settlers disguised as Indians. But however the incident may have begun, there seems no reasonable doubt that the whites participated and carried through to a horrifying conclusion. Protection was promised in order to persuade the besieged to surrender, and when they gave themselves up, all the adults were slaughtered. Seventeen children were distributed among Mormon families, though they were later taken away again by the United States Government and restored to their relatives. Only a few years ago Lee's voluminous diary was published for the first time by the Huntington Library, and though the pages covering the period of the massacre itself have mysteriously disappeared, there are a sufficient number of references to it in later pages to reveal clearly Lee's attitudes. The character of the man makes the whole story far more than a simple tale of raw brutality.

Never since the early days of the New England theocrats had America known a group so afire with the spirit of the prophets and patriarchs as these Mormon settlers. Their religion might strike outsiders as a tissue of absurdities, the practice of polygamy as a gross immorality, and the revelation to the founder, Joseph Smith, one of the crudest hoaxes in the whole history of new religions. But it seemed to inspire its converts with an almost superhuman energy as well as fervor. Not only the government of the community but every detail of daily life was dominated by it. Yet somehow the intense concern with things out of this world went hand in hand with all the worldly virtues of industry, enterprise and prudence. Cities were built, farms flourished, and new country was opened up with astonishing rapidity. Mormons seemed to be tireless as well as competent. To this day even, the fields of a Mormon community seem greener and the houses neater than those of neighboring "gentiles." If, along with all these virtues, went a terrifying self-righteousness, that is not surprising. And as for polygamy, we have it on the authority of no less a philosopher than George Santayana that "to monopolize many women . . . is the dream, conscious or unconscious, of every truly masculine bosom!"

Even among such men, John D. Lee was a leader. He had all the typical qualities to a greater than common degree. Though barely literate, his advice in both spiritual and practical matters was sought and followed. The desperately ill sent for him to ride miles in the middle of the night that he might lay his blessed hands upon them. If they died, it was God's will; if they recovered, it was another demonstration of his superhuman powers. Nor did he fail to prosper as the righteous should. He had many wives and many farms. In fact, it was his usual practice to set up each new wife on a new farm which she managed between the regular visits of inspection he paid to each.

Men of his stamp are more likely than most to receive direct commands from the Lord. Were not the Israelites often commanded to smite the enemies of the chosen people? To any man steeped in the lore of the Old Testament,

The longest ten miles

could there be anything improbable in the command to slaughter infidels, some of whose fellows already had the blood of the chosen on their hands? Lee's diary certainly supports the assumption that it was in this light that he saw the incident. More than once after the tide had turned against him he wrote in effect something like this: Possibly I was wrong. But even so, my conscience is clear. I did what I thought was right and no man need accuse himself for having followed honestly the dictates of his conscience.

News of the massacre soon reached the East, but action was slow, partly because the United States Government had little effective authority so far beyond the frontier, partly because the Civil War was presently to intervene. At his ultimate trial Lee maintained that the massacre had been ordered by Brigham Young, but there is no direct evidence that it was. In any event, the head of the Mormon community repudiated the action, the ringleaders were cast out from the fold, and they scattered to remote places.

Because of the pages missing from Lee's diary, his movements cannot be traced during the years which immediately followed his flight. There is a legend that for several years he was a kindly treated prisoner of the Havasupais in their canyon and that he taught them improved methods of agriculture. By 1872 he was certainly operating the ferry—a large, current-carried boat built of pine which had been hauled sixty miles from the Kaibab forest by oxcart. In that boat, which could transport four wagons at a time, he continued for five years to ferry companies of Mormon immi-

grants on their way to settle northern Arizona. Still bound-
lessly enterprising, he developed a new farm near the
Hopi village, Moenkopi, and another still farther away. Then
finally, the Civil War being past, came the trial and the exe-
cution. All the other defendants were acquitted, but Lee was
executed twenty years after his offense—offered up, as he
maintained, as a scapegoat. For a few years thereafter one
of his wives continued to operate the ferry which then
passed, first to the Mormon church then to Coconino County,
Arizona, in whose hands it remained the only practical crossing of the river until in 1929 it was superseded by the present bridge.

Characteristically, Lee met his fate with unshaken resolu-
tion, a clear conscience, and grim humor. There had never
been anything mealymouthed about his self-righteousness.
Rough talk and a square facing of the facts of life were part
of the tradition he represented. One of his wives was notably vigorous in deed as well as language and was more than
once in trouble with church authorities because of her tendency to direct action and outspoken language. While in
prison awaiting trial, Lee composed a satirical comment inspired by the toughness of the prison beef:

> Old Mormon Bull, how came you here
> We have tuged and toiled these many years.
> We have been cuffed and kicked with sore abuse
> And now sent here for penetentiary use.
> We both are creatures of some note,
> You are food for prisoners and I the scape-goat.

The longest ten miles

There is, so it seems to me, a parallel between John D. Lee and another better known, more respected John who, like him, was executed for assuming the right to slaughter the wicked. History has decided that John Brown murdered on the right side and John Lee on the wrong. History might have turned out differently and John Brown been the criminal, John Lee the martyr. I see no reason to doubt that the two consciences were equally clear.

A mile or two upstream from the ferry a substantial ranch house is now all but abandoned. A mile or two still farther on one comes upon a hydrographical station whose chief lives there with his family, measuring the flow of the river and enjoying a modern version of isolation not so very different from that of John Lee in the old days. But these are only mildly interesting after the drama of the ferry and its history. Leaving John Lee to his conscience—like everything else about him it was robust—the traveler regains the hard, smooth highway and is soon spinning westward at whatever excessive speed he has come to regard as reasonable.

On his left the almost featureless desert level stretches away to the horizon. On his right and close at hand the Vermilion Cliffs raise their thousand-foot bastion of bright-red sandstone. He will skirt their base for many miles and they seem to have been sliced by some great knife—as in fact they were, or at least by something which can cut as cleanly, namely wind and water working where a relatively soft stratum overlays a harder one. These cliffs are what the geologists call Navajo sandstone, a great layer of sedimentary stone still two thousand feet thick in some places and still covering hundreds of square miles, though that is much less than its former extent. It was laid down sometime during the Mesozoic era (the age of the dinosaurs) and perhaps fifty million years after the Permian sea responsible for the Kaibab limestone had retreated.

To the north of the edge we are skirting, Zion Canyon and Rainbow Bridge are fantastic sculpturings in this same formation; to the west, a somewhat earlier but still Mesozoic layer of what once was mud, reveals on an exposed surface the tracks of a dinosaur—one of those huge reptiles descended in the course of many millions of years from the small reptiles or amphibia whose small footprints we saw in the Canyon walls. Go northward into Utah, and the thick layer of Mesozoic rocks which have been washed away from the Canyon area are buried under still later formations, and Bryce Canyon, for example, is sculptured in soft stone of the Cretaceous age, a few million years younger than even the Vermilion Cliffs.

"Must I," so the traveler may ask again as he did at the Canyon, "take all this on faith?" Mostly the answer is again "Yes." Geology is an inductive science, and even the most elementary competence requires the mastery of innumerable details. Nevertheless, the inquisitive layman can, without aspiring to the status of even an amateur geologist, follow the pointing finger of the scientist and observe for himself

The longest ten miles

details which do fit in and thus suggest the general consistency of the geologist's story.

For example: One day near the old Hance cabin and only a few feet from the edge of the south rim precipice I picked up a piece of white limestone, one side of which was coated with half an inch or less of softish red-brown stone. To the uninstructed (i.e., myself a short time before) it would mean nothing—just one kind of rock to which a bit of another kind was adhering. But I had spent an hour searching for it, because I had been told that near here it might be found and that, insignificant as it seemed, it would give the lie to the usual statement that Kaibab limestone (the white part of my specimen) is the youngest rock to be found anywhere in the Canyon or near either of its rims. The soft reddish stone is, in fact, identical with that abundant to the west and gets its name—Moenkopi conglomerate—from the fact that it abounds on the surface at Moenkopi Indian village northeast of Cameron. It is not like the Kaibab, Permian nor, indeed, is it Paleozoic at all. It is older than the Navajo sandstone of the Vermilion Cliffs but belongs nevertheless to the same Mesozoic, or age of the dinosaurs.

Moreover, and as though just to furnish a clear indication that the whole area really was once covered by this material, two small mountains, mesas, or "considerable protuberances" (as Dr. Johnson called the mountains of Scotland) rise improbably above the level of the Kaibab Plateau. The one, called Red Butte, is a few miles south of the Canyon; the other, called Cedar Mountain, a few miles east, each plainly visible from points on the Canyon rim. What are they doing there?

Probably at some idle moment you have noticed a rain-beaten square yard of heavy soil where little inch-high cones of clay, each topped by a pebble, rise as miniature mountains left projecting because the pebble top protected them from the erosion of a heavy rain. This, on a grander scale, is precisely the explanation of Red Butte and Cedar Mountain. The one is crowned by a sheet of lava, the other by a pebbly layer of hard stones. For millions of years these caps have protected them as a small stone protects for a few hours or days a miniature cone of mud from around which the soil has been washed away. And of course, as you will have guessed, Red Butte and Cedar Mountain are composed of the Moenkopi conglomerate of which the last remaining half-inch overlaid the stone fragment I picked up near the Hance cabin.

Often when traveling through one part or another of the great eroded Southwest and seeing the remains of some mountain now reduced to a mere protuberance I have thought to myself: "Well, I got here just in time. A few more hundred thousand years and that vestige of a mountain will no longer be here at all." But the sense of having arrived just in the nick of time was unusually strong as I held in my hand the little fragment of Moenkopi. How rapidly, I wonder, will it go? Must a few thousand or only a few hundred years have to pass before the complete disappearance from

The longest ten miles

the rim of this last bit of local evidence that another great age intervened between the time when the present surface was laid down and the time when the whole area was slowly lifted, when the Mesozoic formations were washed away from the now steeply inclined surface, and the river began to cut downward?

Some twenty miles beyond the river crossing the road passes the western end of the Vermilion Cliffs, and the grade grows gradually steeper as it begins to climb again the Kaibab dome. Here endeth the lesson in Mesozoic geology, and the versatile traveler had best become an ecologist again. As the ground rises, the transition from desert to mountain slope begins to be evident. In August the roadside, where the runoff supplies a little more water, is lined for miles with purple and white cleomes, quite as ornamental as any of the garden varieties. Presently other flowers— red and blue penstemons, pink gilias and white prickly poppies—begin to appear. The grade grows steeper and steeper. Piñon pine gives way to tall ponderosa. And before one has quite reached the top, a heavy forest closes in.

We are still a considerable distance from the boundaries of the Grand Canyon Park but we are within the Kaibab National Forest. At just under eight thousand feet lies a little crossroad center, Jacob Lake, set in a forest clearing. Don't look for the lake which is hard to find and a mere cow pond when found. But do look here for the Kaibab squirrel, sporting its great white plume of a tail. Mostly they are shy creatures and not too often seen elsewhere. Here they have apparently become sufficiently accustomed to man to take him more or less as a matter of course. They won't feed from your hand like the squirrels in a city park but they do not, like their wilder fellows elsewhere, see you first and get away before you have seen them.

If you take the northward branch of the road at Jacob Lake, it will lead you into desert again and to the border of Utah; ultimately, if you persist, to Salt Lake City. Take the southern branch and it brings you after forty-four miles to the northern brink of the Canyon just opposite the point you left two hundred miles and five or six hours ago.

10

The north rim world

On the terrace of the roughstone Lodge which clings to the very brink of the precipice, one may hear the relative merits of the two rims discussed by both novices and aficionados. For one thing, the hotel (Grand Canyon Lodge) is more pretentious—though not, in my opinion, more comfortable—and the greater pretentiousness counts with some travelers. Because of the nearness of the great stone buttes or "temples" cut off from the north rim, the view is more varied, though lacking the grand simplicity of the less broken vista from the south. For this last reason the visitors—and there are, alas, a good many—who never wander far from the terrace get a less clear idea of what it is they are looking at than do those who, at the moment, are staring at them from across the gulf. But of one thing there can be no doubt: take the whole area in, and the north rim is a larger, more varied world in which one may more easily wander farther and get deeper into real wilderness.

This is partly because there are fewer visitors, partly because the whole country to the north is more empty than to the south—because it is, indeed, one of the most sparsely populated and untouched areas of the whole nation. Moreover, nature herself planned on a more generous scale. The north rim is best if you love forests, best for a long succession of spectacular wild flowers; and best for a long stay rather than a short one—for weeks of exploration in a varied and grandiose area.

One enters this special new world as soon as one turns southward from Jacob Lake. For some twenty miles the road cuts through a dense, almost unbroken and grandly evergreen forest, impressive, though to some a bit gloomy. Then the forest retreats up the mountain slopes, leaving the wide valley through which the road runs to a succession of broad alpine meadows where deer and a few cattle graze on flowers rather than grass from spring to autumn. At the crest of the slow rise the altitude is a little over nine thousand feet and the flora is what is often loosely called alpine.

In spring, even the road through the dense forest is lined for mile after mile with blue lupine which may in good years

The north rim world

(like 1957) bloom continuously until fall. Blue is varied by the scarlet of penstemon, the different red of Castilleja and the vivid pink of one of the largest of the gilias. In the meadows there is a gay succession: in spring, acres of white and pink phlox (*P. austromontana*) growing in mats so close to the ground that from a little distance one might take them for patches of lingering snow. Later in the season, after the phlox has disappeared, large blue campanulas, blue penstemon and violet gentians vary the predominant yellow of various daisylike composites.

Within this latitude most of these flowers will not grow below seven or eight thousand feet. They are as distinct even in general appearance from the vegetation at lower altitudes as the atmosphere of mountaintops is from that of the desert. Yet at certain points where a vista opens one may look from the one world down into the other shimmering below. Equally curious is the fact that at the rim one finds at its border an arid zone hardly more than a hundred yards wide. Hot dry air rising from the Canyon bottom, four climatic zones removed, creates a startling "micro climate." Cacti may grow a few minutes walk away from a Canadian forest.

Driving the forty-odd miles of forest and meadow southward from Jacob Lake, one is likely to all but forget the Canyon. As when making the other approach, there is nothing to suggest that anything so extraordinary is again close at hand. After all, one left its brink hours ago. And unless you happen to be one of those rare persons with a built-in compass, you are not likely to have any inner realization that you have been following a great loop which will fall only ten miles short of returning to its starting point. Then suddenly, with no more warning than before, one is at the edge of the precipice again. With good eyes or a pair of binoculars the hotel on the opposite side can be made out; so, and more easily, can a little projection to the left, which is the tower at Desert View twenty-odd miles to the east where one got one's last previous glimpse of the Canyon. On clear days the San Francisco Peaks are visible in the distance and also the broken cone of Sunset Crater. Much closer at hand and directly ahead is the protuberance called Red Butte, the only visible remains of the whole Mesozoic era.

Such landmarks are well worth bearing in mind if one intends to explore even the more accessible scenic lookouts. The north rim follows so tortuous a course, is so given to retreating into bays and jutting out into promontories that orientation is extremely difficult and one finds oneself constantly bewildered. The hotel looks almost due south, the other two most visited spots, Cape Royal and Point Imperial both (though they are more than fifteen miles apart) look eastward toward the junction with the Little Colorado, toward Cameron and, far to the east, the Painted Desert and the Petrified Forest.

Few regions on earth exhibit a more complicated topography within so comparatively small an area. That same elevation of the plateau which was responsible for the Grand (or as it used to be called "Big") Canyon of the Colorado

was responsible for various other strange geomorphic features only comparatively less striking. Not only the Little
Colorado but many other smaller streams eroded their
smaller canyons on their way to join the river, so that a
veritable network of gashes now cuts what was once a plain
peacefully traversed by meandering streams. There are innumerable irregular subplateaus and cliffs. The great river
itself winds a tortuous course, and even the washes which
run only in wet weather repeat on a small scale all the
various phenomena of the river's work.

During the last few years the U.S. Geological Survey
has been busy making new maps, working from the air with
the help of various fixed points established here and there
at ground level. The only existing topographical map is the
result of a survey made more than half a century ago, but
it is astonishingly detailed considering the methods by which
it was made and is worth at least casual study by any
serious visitor curious enough to want to form an idea of
the whole to which the fragmentary views he sees add up.
Nevertheless, adequate map reading requires some training
as well as a better topographical sense than mine. I concluded that I would never really understand the whole
pattern unless I could actually see it. And there is only one
way of doing that—from the air.

Twenty years ago I had taken a little tourist flight in a
rather primitive three-seater which flew over the south rim
hotel and dipped here and there into the Canyon. It was

exciting but more bewildering than clarifying. Most of the time I did not know either where I was or where I had been. What seemed called for now was time and altitude sufficient to give a good bird's-eye view. Also a pilot who would go where I wanted.

A Tucson friend equally anxious to make the trip flew in a chartered plane to the nearest all-weather air strip at Kanab, Utah, some eighty miles away. My wife and I joined her there, and next day we were off for a five and a half hour aerial survey.

Kanab lies just on the southern edge of the red Mesozoic sandstone and hence just beyond the area where the great uplift took place. We followed Kanab Creek's own little grand canyon (colossal in a small way, as Mr. Goldwyn is alleged to have remarked) to the point where it enters the Colorado via a great gash in the big Canyon's walls. Then we followed the north rim westward to the point where the walls fall away and Lake Mead begins. A quick airport lunch at Las Vegas, eaten to the characteristic clank of slot machines and then, leaving that little lake of sin as artificial as Lake Mead itself, we were soon threading our way eastward again, this time along the south rim.

It was a stormy day with half a dozen local showers and thunderheads scattered here and there over the landscape but somehow never just where we were so that the twists and turns of the Canyon were always, and the river itself often, well in view. At the junction with the Little Colorado we followed the latter southward almost to Sun-

set Crater; then back along the precipitous east banks of
the Colorado to Kanab again. As always in an airplane I
kept saying to myself that the makers of relief maps really
were right after all and that I would never have quite
believed it had I lived in any age before this.

During most of the five and a half hour trip no sign of
human habitation was visible. Even Boulder Dam ("highest
in the world," as it is proudly called) is a very insignificant
feature and therefore a salutary reminder that the scale of
man's efforts is still a puny one. Here and there a little green
patch at the mouth of some side canyon signifies the presence of a permanent or semipermanent stream. At Havasu
Canyon a large one represents the successful effort of a
primitive culture to take such advantage of a natural situation as its limited technology permits.

This well-watered little plateau lies about midway between the rim and the river. Just above it Havasu Creek
leaps out of its channel to fall spectacularly a hundred feet
into the milky blue pool at its base. Green covers the little
plateau and creeps a little way up the slope. Probably this
green patch is larger than it was in 1776 when the community, then about the same size as it is today, cultivated
these same fields. A few new food plants have been introduced as well as some improved methods of cultivation.
But that is about all. According to one anthropologist's
study there is no other spot in the United States where a
native culture has retained so much of its aboriginal character.

GRAND CANYON

Time and again we circled the small area and reflected upon the paradoxes of an unprogressive civilization. Unlike the rest of us Americans, the Havasupais have not "conquered nature" or even "controlled it." They have aspired to no more than the ability to live with it, and that has meant so little transformation that from our distance one might have difficulty in deciding whether their oasis was man-made or only an unusually large natural one like a dozen others. They had left and they would have continued to leave the air through which we were nonchalantly flying to the ravens and the eagles. They would never have increased in numbers until only by the "control" and "conquest" of nature could she be compelled to support them.

They have few of our comforts and little or nothing of our artistic or intellectual culture. The men tan deerskins; the women weave baskets. Their religion and their ceremonies are fewer and simpler than those of many other Indian tribes. They treat disease by singing instead of with antibiotics, and I suppose that their average life span is shorter. Yet, their community seems to belong where it is. It is a blessing not a blot on the landscape—which is not a thing that can be said of many communities created by more advanced civilizations.

Man has created some beautiful things—sculptures, paintings, vases and, occasionally, a building. But such beautiful things are few by comparison with the uglinesses he is responsible for, and I do not see how anyone could dispute the statement that the physical world he has taken over is less good to look at because of him or that it grows less and less so from day to day. Most people would, I suppose, maintain that this isn't, after all, so very important. But from an airplane one gets a very detached view, and if Ernest Renan was right in his guess that "The universe is a spectacle which the good God created for his own entertainment," then I am inclined to think He must regard us as having detracted from rather than added to it.

As for man's entertainment rather than God's, that is a different matter and depends upon variable tastes. Even questions of necessity or utility aside, there are still many to whom Lake Mead is an improvement of the landscape from every point of view. What strikes me as the banality of its tidy shore, its speedboats and its aquaplaning bathing beauties is to others more beautiful as well as more entertaining than the natural grandeur of the Canyon or the modest man-made charm of the Havasupai's oasis. It provides "a recreational area" and to those incapable of awe, intellectual curiosity, or aesthetic appreciation "recreation" is the only nonutilitarian activity which has any meaning. That all recreation areas are pretty much alike, that swimming behind Boulder Dam is much like swimming behind any other dam, and that every landscape is much like every other once it has been thoroughly "improved" doesn't matter. The fact that at Boulder the slot machines of Nevada are within easy reach is to them uniqueness enough.

One of the philosophers employed by the Tennessee Valley Authority summed the whole thing up in a sentence

which is a masterly example of the kind of language be-
fitting the attitude: "We must never neglect the development of the recreational potentialities of impounded waters."
And it is surely better to "develop recreational potentialities"
than to do nothing to relieve stark utility. But our civilization is rapidly becoming one in which only two values are
recognized: power and amusement. It would be a pity if
the last refuges where man can enter into another kind of
relation with the natural world should be improved out of
existence by even the most well meaning. The park system
of which Grand Canyon is so striking a part was planned
by men who spoke of "preserving" certain of the grandest
examples of the American continent's natural beauties.
Gradually one has heard less and less about "preserving,"
more and more about "development" and "utilization for
recreation." The two ideals are neither identical nor even
compatible. And it pleases me much to note that since the
above was first written the Park Department has issued a
statement recognizing this point of view.

The sight of Havasu Falls reminded me that though the
geologists say that there are three kinds of waterfalls quite
distinct in their origin I had, so far as I could remember,
seen but two of them. The third, so I had been told, was
represented by the falls of the Little Colorado which none
of my maps recorded but which ought to lie somewhere
within a radius of a hundred miles of Havasu Canyon. The
obvious thing seemed to be to look for these falls, but since

The north rim world

neither I nor the pilot knew where they were, we wandered about a bit before the latter tossed into the air an inquiry: "Where are the falls of the Little Colorado?" Almost immediately, from some plane we never caught sight of, came back the reply: "About eight miles northeast of Sunset Crater." And since Sunset Crater was easy to find, so were the falls. They lie in a rather inaccessible, seldom visited region and they are dry when the river is dry, though on the occasion of our visit a considerable volume of water was tumbling over. But to an inspector of waterfalls (to which position I had just appointed myself) their chief interest lay in the fact that they represent the least common of the three sorts.

Niagara is a grand example of one type. Here a river running across a bed of hard rock suddenly comes to a point where this hard rock gives way to a softer one. Naturally, the soft wears away faster, and presently the river is tumbling from the layer of resistant stone onto that of the less resistant. And Niagara is moving quite rapidly upstream because of another and rather unusual circumstance. The hard layer lies on top of a softer one which the falls themselves undercut until a projecting edge of the hard layer collapses and the brink takes a step backward. It is said to have retreated six miles from the point where it first began—probably toward the end of the last (or perhaps one should say only "the latest") ice age.

In canyon-making country most falls are likely to have, like Havasu, an entirely different origin. When a small

stream flows across the plateau to join a large one, it naturally cuts its canyon more slowly than the larger river.
Hence it finds itself in time running down what is called
"a hanging valley" which ends, not at the river, but high
above it. And there is nothing to do except leap the intervening distance.

The falls of the Little Colorado are, on the other hand,
of the third and least common type. Like Niagara, it is a
whole river, not a tributary to some larger stream into which
it falls. But there is no sudden transition from hard rock to
soft. These falls were created instead by one of those volcanic eruptions which were creating the San Francisco
Peaks. A stream of lava hardened into a "tongue," completely filling the river like a dam. Since this plug obstructed
a canyonlike channel cut many years before, the stream was
now compelled to flow around it and to tumble into the
canyon down one of its side walls. Whether there are in
the Canyon region any examples of the Niagara type I do
not know. But even if there are, they are not necessary to
complete my collection.

Six months after this brief and informal aerial survey, I
made in mid-winter another much more extensive, planned
to cover a large part of the whole southwestern wonderland,
including the Monument Valley region of southern Utah.
Picking up the Colorado River to the west we followed it
down through Glen Canyon where construction has already
started on the dam which will flood some of the wildest

The north rim world

scenery in the entire United States, we flew along the snow-blocked North rim of Grand Canyon, across the low, sun-soaked desert of Death Valley and over the crest of Mount Whitney's fourteen-thousand-foot peak—the highest point on the continent south of Alaska but by plane only a few minutes from the below-sea-level floor of Death Valley. Then we returned to Lake Mead and again picking up the Colorado as it emerges from its imprisonment behind Boulder Dam, followed it to the end of its story at the head of the Gulf of California.

There the great and adventurous river drops the last of the heavy burden of soil, sand and rock-fragments which it has picked up along its course and with a portion of which it is still scouring the Canyon's deepest gorge. The result is a great delta almost blocking its own course to the sea and perhaps destined in time to become an important geological formation as the sand and silt consolidate into stone. Today, while still in the course of formation it is an impressive flood plain across which the river, now broken into meandering streamlets meanders toward its Nirvana in the waters of the Pacific. "Even the weariest river winds somewhere safe to sea."

Such a bird's-eye view of a whole region relates its parts as no other experience can and though it is rather more than most tourists are likely to undertake even a modest flight confined to the immediate neighborhood of the Canyon will abolish the feeling which I at least had always had before—the feeling that I did not know exactly where I was when I had followed one of the minor rim roads to this or that lookout point on the rim itself. Familiar landmarks may tell you in what general direction you are looking, but on your own side the vista is usually closed by some promontory or butte. The result is that you collect a series of more or less discontinuous "views" but little sense of a whole. Knowing where you are helps put them together, even though the familiar saying about Rome applies to the Canyon also. Most people who spend a few hours say to themselves quite sincerely when planning another vacation: "We've already seen Grand Canyon." Those who have visited it many times and accumulated months of exploration get the feeling that they are beginning to know it. Park officials like Chief Naturalist Louis Schellbach who have spent a quarter of a century there are still learning.

Visitors who can be persuaded at least to leave the hotel terrace are encouraged to follow first-class roads to two fine lookouts—Point Imperial and Cape Royal which are, respectively, ten- and twenty-odd road miles from the hotel. The first is northwest, the second somewhat southwest of the tourist center, but because of the meandering outline of the rim both look in a generally eastward direction across the river toward the Painted Desert. Point Imperial is the highest point (8,801 feet) anywhere on either rim, and one may still read quite plainly on a tree which seems to have grown little and healed little the inscription carved into its trunk by

The north rim world

an early exploring party: U.S. Geological Survey. Sept. 3, 1880.

The road to Cape Royal follows the rim pretty closely for a considerable part of its way and there are many glimpses into the Canyon, including some fine sights of the river more than seven thousand feet below and visible for a longer distance than from most points on the south rim. At the Cape itself one narrow peninsula not more than eight or ten feet wide juts far out over the abyss and because it is railed it tempts a good many of even the timid to its dizzy edge.

Resigned to the fact that most visitors neither stay long nor exhibit any very enterprising curiosity, the park authorities do not actively publicize any of the many other little expeditions a day or a half-day long which will take the visitor to spots at least as spectacular and far better suited to the needs of those who get more out of nature when too many others are not looking at her at the same time. Taught, no doubt, by sad experience with automobilists who lose their nerve when asphalt is no longer under their wheels, they exaggerate rather than minimize the minor inconveniences of any deviation from the beaten track. But they will give any information asked for, and it is well to remember that if they say: "Oh I think you can make it," that really means that there is nothing worse than a few miles of more or less primitive dirt road to be anticipated.

A few such roads usually kept in pretty good condition

are marked with modest signs indicating their destination, and though not otherwise publicized they may be taken without further inquiry. Many more, not marked at all, are somewhat casually kept up by the Forest Service, not the Park Department, and are actually intended exclusively for the use of fire fighters who must extinguish a dozen or fifteen forest fires, small or large, in a season. But there is no reason why visitors should not use them, and the fire warden will tell you what condition any one of them is in at the moment. (For such roads, as for all travel off a highway, a four- or five-year-old car is much better than one of the new monsters, because the few inches' greater clearance can make all the difference on a road washed high in the center and with an occasional stone lying where it oughtn't to be.)

Most often used of the secondary unpaved park roads is the one which leaves the main entrance highway about a dozen miles north of the hotel and ends after sixteen miles of slow but not really difficult going at Point Sublime. It is a good intermediate step for those who have "done" the routine points of interest and aspire toward the fire roads which are slightly more advanced. And for its own sake Point Sublime should not be missed.

Perhaps it isn't actually, as I confess it seems to me, the finest vantage point looking over the grandest spectacle which the whole area affords. Perhaps the slight effort one must make to reach it over a road which seems to be leading nowhere as it just manages to squeeze its way between the

The north rim world

trees of a dense forest adds to the value of the view when it bursts upon one. Perhaps the realization that it has been less looked at and less photographed does, too. But even after such enhancements have been discounted, the fact remains that the glorious, the almost appalling splendor, is certainly not surpassed elsewhere.

For one thing, the near view is unusually unrestricted. One looks right and left along the rim which continues far into the distance. For another, the great buttes, characteristic of the north side of the Canyon and rising from the floor between the rim and river, here lie in such positions that long stretches of the river are nevertheless visible.

No other vista I have ever seen at the Canyon or elsewhere gives so much meaning to the well-worn phrase, "magnificent distances." One may see for miles. There is the magnificent distance left and right, the magnificent distance up and down to the river; there is also the magnificent distance up to the great bowl of the brilliant western sky. Yet there is no monotony. Space is diversified though not filled by an endless profusion of shapes and colors—sheer red cliffs, fantastic "temples" in parti-colored stones and, at the very bottom, the red Colorado whose work the whole spectacle is.

Barely visible in a cliff wall not very far below the rim are the ruins of an Indian dwelling which so far no archeologist has excavated, partly because it is so difficult of access. One can only conclude that its builders must have been so desperately pressed that they did not care how hard it would be for them to get out of it, providing they could make it all but impossible for enemies to get in.

What it would mean to live always so precariously perched on the edge of such vast splendor I cannot imagine. To feel very small as one inevitably does at Point Sublime can be an interesting experience as long as you know that before long you will be back where you can feel important again. But to be always a mere speck—something, let us say, like an ant crawling up a cathedral—might be more than the human spirit could endure for long. Our littleness is something we need to be reminded of fairly frequently. But it would be hard to have to face up to it day after day and year after year.

Would it, I wonder, be even harder to bear than that other sort of belittlement to which modern man is being more and more subjected as he is dwarfed by his skyscrapers, made to realize his puniness by comparison with his ever-present machines, and of how little a single solitary individual can count for as the growing crowds of his fellow human beings submerge him?

One cannot be sure of having Point Sublime entirely to oneself. After all, half a dozen or more cars are likely to be making the trip any day during the season. But other passable roads will take one to other less visited spots where one is pretty likely to have the woods and the Canyon to oneself. The Robber's Roost road, for example, is a good one to choose. The gang of horse thieves responsible for its name

The north rim world

departed long ago, leaving only a vague memory, and their ghosts have been laid to rest. It is an interesting spot. Having visited it, one may then go on to the east rim which might well have been made one of the principal sights of the park but just happens to have been left inaccessible to cars except over a poorish road. Here one stands on one of the highest points of the Kaibab dome, and the upper strata have been subjected to such violent erosion that the rim had receded farther than usual from the gorge and one seems to be looking at a valley which has a canyon at its bottom.

During the hours I spent there neither sight nor sound of any human being intruded. And, as so often at isolated spots in the Canyon, I had the queer sense of being out of time. For all anyone who had been suddenly set down here by a time machine could deduce, he might be in any age from the end of the Permian to the present. Had Columbus yet set sail; had Carthage fallen; had, for that matter, man yet made his appearance on earth? Nothing that the eye could see had been affected by any of these events.

I should not have been too much surprised if a pterodactyl had come sailing across the gulf on leathery wings. What actually did appear overhead was a group of three ravens. "Ah," I said to myself, "these are obviously relatively modern times." And it was then that I made a discovery about ravens. They have long had a somewhat sinister reputation which Edgar Allan Poe merely exploited and confirmed. Their voice is far more guttural than that of the crow but

GRAND CANYON

it is no sweeter. In populous places, as I have often noticed, their comments are reminiscent of Cowper's jackdaw and they sometimes provoke the same reflection:

> There is a bird who by his coat
> And by the hoarseness of his note,
>   Might be supposed a crow;
> A great frequenter of the church,
> Where bishop-like he finds a perch,
>   And dormitory too.
>
> . . . .
>
> He sees that this great roundabout
> The world, with all its medley rout,
>   Church, army, physic, law,
> Its customs and its businesses
> Is no concern at all of his,
>   And says—what says he?—"Caw."
>
> Thrice happy bird! I too have seen
> Much of the vanities of men,
>   And sick of having seen 'em
> Would cheerfully these limbs resign
> For such a pair of wings as thine
>   And such a head between 'em.

But in lonely places the tone of the raven's comment seems to change, though I am willing to admit the possibility that the change is more in my attitude than in his. But, however that may be, there is no doubt that when no other living thing is about, he begins to seem almost companionable. His caw or his croak seems less a jeer, more like a friendly hail as he passes, sometimes high overhead intent on business of his own, sometimes swooping low as though deigning to take some interest in the earth-bound creatures who have intruded upon him.

It is a lonesome sound, so most people say. But not so lonesome as no sound other than the wind in the trees or the rattle of a stone which has waited millions of years for this particular moment when it has been ordained that the Canyon shall be widened by precisely its half-inch width. At least the raven is, like us, a creature confined to a narrower band of time and, like us, conscious of certain things whether he be conscious of time or not. I am almost ready to swear that what I have heard him call was: "Hi there, fellow creature!"

11

The most ancient inhabitants

Shiva Temple is one of the largest of the buttes which time and water have separated from the north rim. It rises some four thousand feet from the base, its flat top covers about three hundred acres, and until 1937 it had never—so far as anyone then knew—been climbed. In that year scientists from the American Museum of Natural History organized an expedition to penetrate its supposed mysteries. Erosion had made Shiva an island many thousand years ago—twelve to thirty-five, guessed some geologists, though one member of the expedition spoke hopefully of a possible hundred thou-

The most ancient inhabitants

sand. What might not possibly be found living there in safe isolation?

"Dinosaurs!" suggested one newspaper writer, disregarding the fact that the last dinosaur had presumably died millions of years before there was a Canyon, much less a butte later detached from it. But if, in sober fact, the isolation was as old as the last ice age, then either plants and animals elsewhere extinct might still survive there or distinct species might have evolved—like those which Darwin, not yet an evolutionist, was astonished to find limited to single islands in the Galápagos group. One member of the 1937 expedition said: "There is no reason why small animals isolated aeons ago should have become extinct. . . . If we are able to compare this flora and fauna with that of the Canyon's main rim, we would have a time clock telling us approximately the number of years it has taken to bring about structural change. It will be rolling back the curtain of time to glimpse life as it was in prehistoric days." To a biologist this was indeed an exciting prospect, and the expedition was elaborate, complete with an airplane to drop supplies to the hardy explorers.

Not unnaturally the newspapers took up the story and ran away with it. Reporters on the rim kept in communication by radio and were ready to break the exciting story to a waiting world. But, alas, the bubble soon burst and the whole enterprise turned into a slightly comic fiasco. The scientists spent ten days on Shiva. They found familiar cacti, mice, chipmunks and unmistakable evidence of coyotes and ring-tailed cats. Instead of species new to science, they found also primitive tools and ornaments to prove that Indians had spent some time there, probably in the days before the white man came. In other words, the "isolation" of Shiva was a myth. Animals had found it no more difficult to climb than the scientists had. And except for this fact nothing new was discovered.

Almost exactly a year later a geologist poking about in the depths of the Canyon near the top of the inner gorge came across a single bit of sedimentary rock which, all by itself, disproved an assumption of long standing and suggested revision of the timetable for organic evolution. What he found has not, so far as I know, been found again. Had the searcher not been lucky, even the knowledge which enabled him to recognize the importance of his discovery would have done him no good. Once more, as has so often been the case, a modicum of serendipity served him better than the explorers of Shiva had been served by all their planning.

What the geologist found was the clear imprint of a medusa or jellyfish, essentially similar to those which float by millions in today's oceans. Jellyfish have no skeletons and hence make no true fossils. But imprints like this one are not uncommon in very old rock, and from such evidence jellyfish are known to be among the oldest forms of life of which any clear record has been left. But no previous bit of evidence was so old as this. The fragment of stone came from the geologic formation known as the Algonkian which,

The most ancient inhabitants

at the Canyon, was deposited in successive layers on top of volcanic basalt after the latter had sunk below a later sea. This puts it back more than, say, 500,000,000 years, into what was for long called the Proterozoic era—precisely because the only traces of life formerly found so far back in time had appeared to be the remnants left by lowly plants much like the modern algae. The assumption had been that the only animals then existing were the one-celled protozoa which had no skeletons to fossilize and were too small to leave recognizable imprints.

But it is a long way from a protozoan to a jellyfish. The latter is not only multicelled but, relatively speaking, very complex and highly developed. Its body is differentiated into various specialized organs. It even has a nervous system. Hence vast stretches of time and many intermediate organisms of gradually increasing complexity must have intervened between it and the lowly protozoan. But until this single imprint was found, the earliest clear evidence of animal life at the Canyon was in the Cambrian rocks of the Paleozoic era during the early part of which trilobites became the dominant animals.

Because these primitive ancestors of the crustaceans and the insects had hard external shells, their fossil remains survived by millions. But because creatures intermediate between the protozoa and the jellyfish had developed neither chitin nor the silica or lime "skeletons" characteristic of still higher organisms, they rarely left traces. But as the discovery of a single jellyfish in the Algonkians seems to prove, the seas must have been swarming with creatures far more complex than protozoa long before the end of the Protozoic era.

What difference does this fact make in our general conception of the evolution of life? At least it helps the imagination fill an enormous gap. But this is not all. It contributes to that revision of the timetable which has been going on rapidly during the decade or two just past. And most of the revisions, no matter by what method they are decided upon, take the same general direction, which might be summed up thus: Everything seems to point to the conclusion (1) that life, even fairly highly organized life, is older than was formerly supposed and (2) that modern man, the species of the genus homo to which we belong, is much younger than he used to be thought. Man seems to have had a longer prehistory as animal and a shorter history as man than was believed only a few years ago.

The Algonkian jellyfish from the depths of the Canyon is a unique specimen and it has been dead for no one knows just how many hundreds of millions of years. A different animal just as interesting in its own way and for reasons somewhat similar has several times been found very much alive in temporary pools near the Canyon's rim. It is a little creature an inch or two long which looks rather like some kind of crustacean but is so primitively ambiguous that classifiers are doubtful whether it ought to be called crustacean or, perhaps, "arachnid" (spider- and scorpionlike

The most ancient inhabitants

animal) instead. In this respect as well as others it suggests the trilobites which have been extinct for many millions of years. In fact, if it were known only from the Paleozoic, that would seem reasonable enough and structurally it would have been little if any in advance of its fellows. Yet it is very much alive, in fact still extraordinarily tenacious of life, in this twentieth century of the Christian era.

Apus aequalis, as science calls this stubborn little anachronism, is in much the same situation as Wordsworth's Lucy. It dwells among untrodden ways and it is a creature whom there are very few to love and none at all to praise—unless you count a few biologists especially interested in the early stages of evolution. It doesn't get so much as a mention in most zoology textbooks unless they are very inclusive indeed. Yet it belongs to a family so old that the cockroach (often cited as deserving to be honored for its ancient lineage if for nothing else) is by comparison a mere parvenue. Insects much like the modern cockroach have been around only since the middle of the Paleozoic; creatures much like Apus for perhaps a hundred million years longer. In that remote day Apus had many relatives. But in all the close collateral branches except one the ancient line is long extinct.

Apus was first noticed as occurring near the Canyon rim in October, 1939, when he turned up in a temporary pool of water. But he has been observed several times since. His appearances anywhere are usually brief but they may occur in many different places—after an unusually hard rain in a burning desert of the American Southwest or on top of a rocky hillock in central Australia. Sometimes he is so abundant in Mexico as to be used for food. But usually he appears and then disappears. In fact, if the secret of his surprising appearances and disappearances were not known, he might be used as an argument for "spontaneous generation" and assumed to be born, as so many creatures were once thought to be, of mud and putrefaction.

The explanation of the mystery lies in the extraordinary persistence of some spark of life in an egg which can endure for unbelievably long periods and under what seem like impossible conditions. Paleontologists say that fossils so close to the modern Apus that they must be considered members of the same genus are well over a hundred million years old. But what is even more important is the fact that they belonged to a very ancient group even then and that their habits as well as their structure and the stages of development through which the young go seem to correspond very closely with those of the trilobites. What goes on in a pool which has called Apus into life must be very like what went on in a Cambrian sea.

What gives especial piquancy to the appearance of Apus near the rim of the Canyon is the fact that in the Tonto rocks of the Cambrian age lie the fossilized shells of his near relatives which lay buried under three thousand feet of later sediments until they were exposed by the down-cutting knife of the river in comparatively recent times.

They—so far as the record goes—disappeared off the face

The most ancient inhabitants

of the earth nearly 200,000,000 years ago. Apus, who may not have existed as such when the trilobites flourished, was nevertheless constructed upon the same plan. Both are the model T's of animate creation. And with the exception of one other close relative, no other creature with jointed legs is so much of an anachronism

Why did the trilobite die and Apus remain so persistently alive? It is easy to say that the former, like so many other creatures, perished either because the end of a geological age brought great changes in the conditions which living creatures had to meet or because, after flourishing for so many millions of years, it found itself at last unable to compete successfully with other organisms which had been progressive enough to evolve while it thought that the old ways were good enough. But what has Apus got that a trilobite didn't have? Why did he, though built on the same old-fashioned model, manage to survive geological change and the competition of cleverer animals?

In the eastern United States Apus does indeed appear to have become extinct. At least it has never, so far as I know, been noticed there, though it is to be found in many other places. By way of compensation a rival claimant to the title of "oldest surviving type of jointed animal" swarms up Atlantic beaches from New England to Yucatan, though it is absent from our Pacific coast as well as from all Europe. The horseshoe crab (which isn't a crab) is familiar to most seashore visitors, who have probably seen it stranded upside down on its large dome-shaped carapace, waving its spidery legs, and perhaps thrashing about with its long pointed spike of a tail. It has existed, apparently unchanged, since the early Mesozoic—which is to say since about the same time as the first known fossils of the genus Apus. But, like Apus again, the type to which it belongs is much older, and very similar animals were flourishing in the early Paleozoic. Its larva are strikingly similar to the fossilized larva of trilobites, and like Apus again it is ambiguously arachnid or crustacean. But what is most puzzling is that, like Apus, it is still about when it shouldn't be. It has somehow eluded the general law: change or die.

Such living fossils have been recognized for a long time and are to be distinguished, of course, from merely ancient forms that have survived as whole genera or even families. Jellyfish, for example, are older than Apus or any of its relations, and there are many, many different species. In such a case the general model was obviously good enough to compete in its humble way with more advanced designs. But a true living fossil is one which alone, and for no apparent reason, is still here while all or nearly all of its once flourishing relatives have succumbed. Trilobites were good enough to survive for millions of years before they were liquidated, though in the end they were. Apus triumphs over time.

The classic examples are, for the most part, survivors from ages much less remote. There is, for instance, the ginkgo tree, sole survivor of a once numerous group and especially in-

The most ancient inhabitants

teresting to botanists because it is the only plant still extant which establishes a certain important link between the spore bearers, like ferns, and the seed bearers which came later. Alone among flowering plants its reproductive sperm is motile like that of the ferns, instead of passive like the pollen of all other flowering plants. Its ancestors were once among the most conspicuous of all trees, covering much of the earth. In fossil form it is known in the United States as well as in many other places. But it survived only in China, probably under the protection of cultivation. And yet it is also so far from delicate that few other trees can endure as well the hard conditions of city life.

Parallels in the animal kingdom are the platypus and its somehow less famous relation, the spiny anteater, only survivors of the earliest mammals which, like them, continued to lay eggs after the fashion of birds and reptiles though they had already evolved that stupendous mammalian invention, milk-producing glands. But they are less of a mystery than some other less striking living fossils, because their isolation in Australia from competing mammals more advanced than the still relatively primitive marsupials, made life easier for them than it was for their compeers in other lands. Besides, the platypus and the spiny anteater are obviously very near to extinction.

Most exciting of all such improbable survivors are those whose fossil ancestors were well known but which were assumed to be long and totally extinct as a class until some representative which had eluded discovery unexpectedly turned up very much alive. Very recently three such—one plant and two animals—have thus, as it were, come back from the dead.

Paleontologists had for some time been familiar with the fossilized ancestor of the California redwood and had given it the generic name, Metasequoia. But no one was more surprised than they when a few specimens turned up in the interior of China. And though the last survivors in the wild have by now probably been cut down, the race has been saved from extinction by seedlings which seem to be doing very well in various public and private arboreta in this country.

Of the two recently recognized animals the New Zealand lizard, tuatara, had been known but unappreciated for more than a century before it was recognized as belonging to a class of reptiles which flourished during the early part of the Mesozoic but were presumed to have disappeared or at least become very rare almost as long ago as the dinosaurs. Even more startling because previously totally unknown, was the fish now called Latimaria, which was so obviously unlike anything they had ever seen before that the fishermen who took it in their net off the South African coast sent it on to a local museum. It is very closely similar to a fossil, also from the Mesozoic but supposed to have become extinct as a group toward the end of that epoch. And the most obvious moral of all this is that you can never be quite sure what actually is "as dead as the dodo." The lizard tuatara is being carefully protected in its native habitat but even so its future

The most ancient inhabitants

outside zoos is probably not too bright. On the other hand, several Latimaria have been taken since the first one, and for all anyone knows this fugitive from the Cretaceous may be doing pretty well in the depths of the sea.

Romancers (especially since the success of Conan Doyle's *Lost World*) are especially fond of dinosaurs, and one figures prominently in a popular comic strip as the pet of some sort of cave man. "If," one may hear their creators saying, "a contemporary of the giant reptiles has just turned up, then why is it absurd to suggest that a diplodocus may also be living in some remote corner of the earth? Why laugh so merrily at the several respectable citizens of a western state who reported just a year or two ago that they had caught glimpses of a small dinosaur in the wild—after their imaginations had been stimulated by an amateur's guess that certain obviously fresh bones found in a cave looked like those of just such a creature?" To these queries there are two answers. In the first place, even a small dinosaur is rather large to escape detection. In the second place (and more importantly), large animals are far less likely than the smaller ones to find niches into which they can fit. But neither of these answers is likely to be very convincing to those who would rather not be convinced.

As to the heady rumor that a descendant of Neanderthal man may be surviving in the Himalayas, that rumor was assured a long life by the genius who conferred upon the hypothetical subhumans the unforgettable name, Abominable Snowman.

GRAND CANYON

Someday, I hope, I may see for myself the Apus shrimp (which isn't a shrimp) flourishing briefly in some pool which temporarily fills a depression in that Kaibab sandstone laid down at just about the time when the trilobite was making his last stand. I should like to see him clothed in the curious shell that looks old-fashioned even to the layman's eye and swimming on his back as the trilobites are believed to have done and as the young of the horseshoe crabs still do. It is the nearest any man can come to peering into a Paleozoic sea.

So far, however, I have never had that good luck. Despite the persistence of the race through time and the persistence of the resting eggs through years of desperately unfavorable conditions, the active life of Apus is short, and he is so surprisingly cranky that he is said to be difficult to keep even in laboratory aquaria. As an individual he is here today and gone tomorrow.

A year and a half ago I went even to the length of extracting from Mr. Schellbach, then chief naturalist at the Canyon, a promise that if Apus appeared at a time when I was not there, he would wire me the news so that I might (literally) fly to see for myself. But either this was not an Apus year or no one noticed that it was. To date, therefore, I have seen him only in two forms: dismally pickled in a bottle and, much more interestingly, preserved in a different way.

A month or two ago I happened to be in Mr. Schellbach's laboratory when I noticed on a table a few feet away a fragment of what looked like red shale bearing several beautifully preserved fossils of some arachnid or crustacean. As I moved over to examine it more closely, it came to the tip of my tongue to ask, "Hermit shale?" But something familiar in the shape of the "fossils" checked me in time. The shale was actually a piece of hardened mud which, if left *in situ*, might possibly have become shale a good many millennia hence. The "fossils" were Apus which had sunk a bit into the drying mud as the evaporation of water from a temporary pool had condemned them to death. Probably the mud had dried only a few months before. But I have never seen a neater demonstration of the way fossils are made. From a few feet away this fossil-to-be looked very much as though it might be two or three hundred million years old.

In very much the same way the only jellyfish known from the Proterozoic era had happened to leave his imprint in the mud which was to become an Algonkian rock. It had to wait a long time for someone to find and recognize it.

12

The balance of nature

Thomas Henry Huxley, improving on a hint from Darwin, once propounded a sort of riddle. The prosperity of the farmer's clover crop depends, so he said, upon the number of old maids in the British Isles.

Pretty farfetched, you think. Actually, not so much so as you can be forgiven for supposing. The explanation goes like this: Clover blossoms set seed only if they have been fertilized by bumble bees—which need to be very abundant. Field mice eat the larvae of bumble bees, but cats cut down the number of field mice. Old maids are notoriously prone to

The balance of nature

keep cats. Ergo, the more old maids, the more cats; the more cats, the fewer field mice; the fewer field mice, the more bumble bees, and the more bumble bees, the more clover.

Nobody is likely to propose that any department of agriculture undertake to discourage marriage as a way of improving the clover crop. Many have, however, advocated the elimination of cats for many different reasons—including the simple reason that they don't like them. Others have argued that fewer cats would mean more birds, and that more birds would mean fewer insects. But fewer cats would much more certainly mean more mice, and mice can be very destructive. Where would the balance lie? Nobody really knows, and the results of even the best intentioned tampering with a natural plant and animal association are always difficult to predict.

Consider, for example, a Grand Canyon case in point. One of the earliest white residents of the region was a certain Uncle Jose Owens, an old-time hunter who put up a sign "Cougars [or Mountain Lions] killed to order" and he is said to have had a record of 1,100 slain. Probably neither he nor any of those who employed him had any idea that the near extermination of the lions would have any effect other than the elimination of one more species of "vermin." To this day the state of Arizona pays a bounty for every one of them slain—though not in Grand Canyon National Park. And though cougars are, it is hardly necessary to say, not vegetarians, one result of their near disappearance has been the laying waste not only of hundreds of square miles of a once flourishing plateau clothed with many different shrubs and small trees but also, in places, serious damage to actual forests.

In this case there is only one connecting link between cougars and trees—namely deer. There were never too many of them when there were mountain lions enough. Neither was there any danger that the mountain lions would exterminate the deer. Though they did not lie down together, they did, nevertheless, in a sense, get on very well. Nor was the vegetation which protected the soil against erosion disastrously thinned by a mounting deer population driven by near starvation to eat the shrubbery to the ground and desperately to gnaw the bark from dying trees.

Ask the biologist on the south rim to show you the quarter-acre area not far from the main road which was experimentally fenced in nearly thirty years ago. Thirty years is a very short time in the history of any natural region, yet the quarter acre protected by a fence does not seem to belong with the area outside. Nor is it merely a matter of the degree to which plant life is flourishing. Outside, various species—some of them among the handsomest—have completely disappeared. You would never guess that only thirty years ago the Gambel oak and the beautiful cliff rose flourished all about, though they are now to be seen only where the deer cannot get at them. Outside even the sagebrush is in a dying condition, and the junipers have no branches low enough for a deer to reach. Every winter thousands of them come into the park to carry the destruction of the range land one step further and then to die of starvation. A few thousand of the mountain lions slaughtered over the years would solve the problem. But their numbers have now been reduced below the level at which they can rebuild the population and, desirable as it would be, they cannot be reintroduced because of the protests that would arise, not only from ranchers in contiguous areas but also, probably, from those who want the deer "protected"— even if protection means that they will starve slowly to death during the winter.

Most of man's ignorant and disastrous interventions in nature's far from simple plan have been in his own supposed interest, but his disinterested attempts to improve upon the existing situation from the standpoint of the fauna and flora themselves have often been worse than unsuccessful. So it was in the case of the Grand Canyon deer where the best of intentions went so disastrously awry that they taught a lesson wildlife managers will not soon forget.

Fifty years ago there were already too many deer because of the men who thought they were furthering their own interests by eliminating the predators. But deer are among the most attractive of animals; visitors like to see them around; and it was natural that park authorities should want to protect them still more. Hence, in 1906, a section of the Kaibab forest region stretching northward from the north rim was declared a national game preserve, and a systematic campaign began to rid the region entirely of the wicked predators. Wolves were completely exterminated. More than seven hundred mountain lions, nearly five thousand coyotes, more than five hundred bobcats and many eagles were killed. For a time thereafter the deer increased at the rate of about 20 per cent a year. When the campaign began, the herd was estimated at four thousand. Twelve years later the food supply was visibly declining, but the policy of "protection" continued. By 1924 seventeen hundred deer might be seen in a single meadow, and the size of the total herd was estimated at one hundred thousand.

Now, there is serious doubt whether the "Malthusian law" which Darwin made one of the cornerstones of his theory of natural selection really does work in a state of nature. If it did, we ought to see in every forest, desert and jungle throngs of nearly starving animals. For some reason we do not, and what we do usually see is a nice balance between population and food supply. But there is no doubt that "the Malthusian law" does work when either a human or an animal population is protected against natural checks. It works in China and India, for example, where hundreds of thousands are in constant danger of starvation. Given as much time as it has had in these countries, the law may begin to work in Europe and the United States also, even though techniques of food production have so far kept one jump ahead of increasing need. And it most certainly did work in the Grand Canyon Game Preserve. Had the deer been capable of the typical human attitude, they would have said to one another, "Watch us grow. We have triumphed over our enemies. The new era of permanent prosperity has begun."

As a matter of fact, however, it was just ending. That very

winter the food supply failed. Thousands upon thousands of deer died, and as one observer reported it, "those that lived nibbled at every leaf and twig till the whole country look^ed as though a swarm of locusts had swept through it, leaving the range (except for the taller shrubs and trees) torn, gray, stripped and dying." In many areas, it was said, 80 to 90 per cent of the forage was gone. Then the whole region was reopened to hunting—but for the hunting of predators as well as of deer. The physically degenerate population continued to die, and by 1930 the hundred-thousand herd had been reduced to about twenty thousand, many of them in very poor condition. What the general situation now is over the whole Kaibab area I do not know, but within the park there are again too many deer and no important predators to keep them down. What is worse, the vegetation of the south rim at least has deteriorated seriously and perhaps permanently. It is closer now to desert than it was when we began to "protect" it.

The sportsmen (or killers for the fun of killing) like to think that they have the answer. No other group has so persistently promoted the policy of extermination of all predators, because they go on the theory that the fewer "game animals" killed by "vermin," the more there will be for them to kill by their own methods. But it does not always work that way and there is, besides, another catch. Hunters kill only at random or, what is worse, pick out the finest specimens. Predators, on the other hand, take first the sick and the overaged. Hence, a population kept down by predators tends to maintain its vigor; a population thinned by hunters tends to degenerate.

Where the human population is small, the number of animals killed by the hunter does not have much effect; where the population is large, it becomes the dominating factor. Constantly accumulating evidence demonstrates that, almost without exception, the predators serve to maintain the health of the very populations they prey upon by protecting them against the Malthusian law and at the same time keep similarly in check the enemies of other species so that a balance is established which cannot be upset at any point without repercussions ending no one can quite say where. Yet despite all this, both the national government and many state governments allow themselves to be persuaded by the hunters that the slaughter of many species of owl and hawk as well as of nearly all the carnivores, is a laudable public service.

Unfortunately but not ununderstandably, the hunters are supported or at least not opposed by a group which by now should be learning better. Those who have been awakened to a sympathetic interest in wild creatures and who would like to share the earth with them are likely to begin as partisans of the seemingly more innocent and, by our standards, more attractive. They are shocked by the sight of a striking hawk; terrified by the image of a cougar's pounce. Almost inevitably they first think in terms of "the innocent" and "the guilty." Though the vast majority of them are carnivores themselves, they do not usually remember that. But there always remains

The balance of nature

the problem of the world we never made, of the world of nature where to eat is hardly less inevitable than to be eaten.

That fact we are bound to recognize intellectually and to it we need to make some sort of emotional adjustment. The naturalist, W. H. Hudson, said he made it his rule never to intervene in nature, either to kill or to rescue. Perhaps it is not necessary to be quite so austere. It would be inhuman not to protect a pet, perhaps only somewhat less so not to save an individual songbird from a hawk. Such acts as these represent the protest of what is possibly our higher human nature against the scheme from which we struggle to detach ourselves. But we cannot detach ourselves completely, and most assuredly we cannot revise radically the whole scheme. Unless we do accept it, we certainly cannot preserve in anything like their native states the areas we have set aside for just that purpose. The predator is an essential part of nature's plan which is not a pure "social union" though it is also not merely red in tooth and claw. Moreover, it seems almost miraculously effective in maintaining a vigor which tends to diminish as soon as we effectively intervene at any point.

If you think, as the geologist does, in terms of hundreds of millions of years, then great races of animals and the vegetations amid which they live do come and go. They multiply, improve their techniques of offense and defense, multiply vastly in numbers and finally, having had their day, vanish off the face of the earth. But in terms of humanly conceivable time, the flora and fauna of most regions remain astonishingly stable. Once man takes a hand, the picture changes with terrifying rapidity. Animals plentiful in one man's youth become extinct during the lifetime of his children. Forests give way to fields and also, alas, to wastes. Hills are washed away because of the timber cut; arid prairies turn into deserts.

But until man does interfere, centuries pass with little change. The mountain lions kill the deer, and the deer browse upon the vegetation. Yet the deer do not become extinct, and the vegetation continues to flourish. The stable balance is something enormously complex of which we usually see only some spectacular element like that of the carnivore versus the herbivore. One marvels both that this balance can be so easily upset by man and, what is even more striking, that when all the delicate checks and counterchecks are left to themselves, they maintain successfully their intricate interrelationships. Somehow they do. And the moral for either the exploiter or the conservationist is this: If you are going to change that balance, be very sure you know what you are doing—which in fact you usually don't.

Whenever man is using land primarily to produce food, problems arise. Very different ones are faced in a national park where the intention is to preserve nature herself, and much less interference is necessary or desirable. In fact, the real problem in natural areas becomes primarily the problem of preventing those interferences with the natural balance which the presence of many visitors introduces. To take a simple example, there is the problem created by the tourists who feed the increasingly tame deer in the most frequented area. The diet is bad, and the deer become so accustomed to having the food supplied to them that they become definitely a beggar class, incapable of feeding themselves when the winter sets in and the tourists depart. That minor problem is fairly well solved by a simple practice. Every so often, before they are completely corrupted, the deer are moved away to remoter areas, and a new group drifts in.

Quite frequently it is the "cute" animals who create problems under even the slightly unnatural conditions of a park. Take, for instance, the chipmunks and the ground squirrels. No creature is more endearing, and the fact that some species eat the flower stalks of the agave, a spectacularly beautiful flowering plant, is not serious so long as the ground squirrel population is kept down by foxes. But once the fox has been exterminated, the agave also is threatened with extinction. Even the trays of seed put out to attract birds for the benefit of visitors mean that the chipmunks who come uninvited multiply so alarmingly that they, like the beggar deer, have to be periodically transported to remoter areas where artificial overpopulation is not a problem.

While park biologists are making such minor efforts to restore the balance which man's activities have upset, thousands of more delicate adjustments, some known but many more yet unrecognized, are being made by nature herself whose "warfare" of species against species has the paradoxical effect of maintaining a status quo. Her "mechanisms" (even assuming that they are no more) simulate an almost perfectly calculated intervention, checking organisms which seem on the point of getting out of hand while relieving the pressure upon others threatened with extinction.

A few years ago a ranger on the south rim noticed a number of unfamiliar "caterpillars" eating the leaves of certain trees. He took them in to Chief Naturalist Louis Schellbach who recognized them immediately as not caterpillars at all but the larvae of some kind of sawfly—that is, of one of those rather formidable-looking insects with gauzy wings and a long ovipositor which looks so much like a sting that the layman often gives the insects a wide berth.

Now, there are many different kinds of sawflies with so many different ways of life that it is difficult to say offhand whether man should regard certain of them as friend or foe. Some destroy definitely obnoxious insects, but others destroy other insects regarded as beneficial because they keep down still other obnoxious species. The whole thing is so complicated that in some cases only nature could untangle the web, and it was probably for this reason that Mr. Schellbach decided to rear the larvae and find out to what species they belonged. He started with fifty. Nine died a natural death somewhere along the line; a few were killed at various stages as specimens to illustrate the course of the development. Twenty reached the last stage before the emergence of the adult. But only five sawflies emerged.

Out of the other fifteen came small two-winged flies of a species not yet determined. Their parent had been a parasite on the sawfly, as many sawflies are parasites on still other

The balance of nature

insects—doing notable work, for instance, in keeping down the population of certain large destructive caterpillars. Great fleas have little fleas to bite 'em. But the point in this case is that it seemed reasonably sure that the park authorities had no cause to worry about serious damage from the sawfly. Its two-winged predator appeared to have the situation well in hand.

Or take a more spectacular illustration. Driving one spring morning through the beautiful high-altitude forest near the north rim, I was horrified to see every tree in a fine aspen grove mangled by some sort of tent caterpillar whose unsightly webs made it all too evident that a great many of them were at work. Were the aspens doomed to extinction or chronic disfigurement? I reported to the biologist, who knew all about the situation and knew that though the trees would this year be for a while despoiled of their beauty, they would presently be clothed with new leaves and that next year the infestation would be less. Nature, unlike man, is too "wise" to permit a species to become so "successful" as to endanger its own existence by destroying the environment upon which its life depends.

The story is this: The moth into which these caterpillars will turn lays its eggs in the fall. They half-hatch, then go into a state of suspended animation so that they are ready to emerge just in time to eat the first tender leaves of spring. This seems a dangerously clever device, and they employ also an even cleverer one. They feed at night while they are safe from birds and retire to their tents during the hours when birds are eating them and their kind. Most birds won't tear into the tents, although (just so the species won't have everything its way) the cuckoos will and they destroy a certain number. Before long the surviving caterpillars have had their fill and retire into cocoons while the aspens put out a second set of leaves.

Now, if these caterpillars—like many, many insects—had two or more broods a year so that another came along to eat the aspen's second set of leaves, then the situation would be serious. But, as though they "knew" it would be disastrous to "overgraze" the trees, they do not crop them again until next year. Would that men in the Southwest were as knowledgeable about the dangers of overgrazing! Live and let live is the caterpillar's motto. Besides, there will be next year a lesser infestation because the caterpillar is parasitized by a sawfly; because a big population of the one means a flourishing population of the other; and hence, because this year the caterpillar population will be drastically reduced.

Man, who likes to think that only his welfare and indeed only his tastes should count, is inclined to regard all such arrangements as unnecessarily complicated. Since he is mildly pleased by trees, he doesn't see why it is necessary to have caterpillars to eat them and then sawflies to keep down the caterpillars. Why not just have no caterpillars to begin with? Nature's scheme seems rather too much like that of the old man's in *Alice*:

The balance of nature

But I was thinking of a plan
To dye one's whiskers green
And always use so large a fan
That they could not be seen.

Why dye them green in the first place?

On man's own egotistical assumptions the question is a good one. But he is the only creature who makes it, and he might as well face the fact that "Nature's children all divide her care." Perhaps man is her most remarkable achievement. But perhaps also—as some mystic might suggest—she is less concerned about him than about some of her others, now that he has so confidently taken things into his own hands and boasts that at last he is "conquering nature." Obviously, she prefers her own system of balance in which cougars as well as deer and caterpillars as well as aspens and sawflies all flourish. Why? Is it because she loves variety for its own sake or because it is by the endless variety of her experiments that she has brought life to its present state of development and that she intends to go on with the experimentation, giving each creature a chance to see what it can make of itself? After all, the mammals didn't look very promising back toward the end of the Mesozoic when they got their start.

Even if you take the mechanistic evolutionist's point of view and say only that this is the way things happened (or rather couldn't help happening), the fact remains that nature's complicated plan works. It keeps the world full of an infinite variety of things and makes it a great deal more interesting than it would be if we had it all our own way. And decidedly we do not have it all our own way. We are not outside but part of the system of checks and balances.

Once, after a panel discussion of the meaning of conservation broadcast from a local Tucson station, an excited fundamentalist telephoned in to denounce me as blasphemous because I seemed to deny that man, the only creature with a soul, had been given dominion over the beasts and was therefore not only permitted but required to use them exclusively for his own purposes. Only man, she said, was valuable in God's sight, whereas I had put myself on the devil's side when I had confessed that I should not like to see even such "noxious" creatures as the tarantula and the scorpion totally exterminated.

She was silenced (but I am afraid not convinced) when I pointed out that, on the evidence of the Bible itself, this had not always been God's point of view. He did not say to Noah, "Save as many men as you can and let the soulless beasts drown." He said instead something like this: "You and your family are enough to preserve your species. Get two of every other so that none shall become extinct." And he didn't say only the "useful" ones, either. The tarantula and the scorpion must have been taken along. And what right have we to exterminate what God took the trouble to save in the Ark?

It is only within the confines of an area set aside for a specific purpose that we can any longer preserve in an almost

The balance of nature

unmodified state the beautiful balance achieved through nature's far from simple plan, and that is perhaps the strongest reason why such areas should be kept as natural as it is possible to keep them. To do so it is rarely necessary to interfere except to redress the balance after man himself has upset it. Seldom indeed under natural conditions does one species threaten the existence of another. Genocide is a human invention, and only man commonly wages wars of extermination. Moreover, though to eat and be eaten is certainly a law of nature, we are learning that it is neither the only law nor alone responsible for the maintenance of the balance.

In some curious way not entirely understood both plants and animals to some extent regulate their own population. Many birds, for example, will lay a second and third set of eggs if the first is destroyed. Obviously the total number they are capable of producing is not normally produced, and this "self-control" makes unnecessary all the brutality of elimination by starvation or by the spontaneous increase in the predator population which early evolutionists assumed to be the only checks on immoderate increase in the numbers of given species. Similarly, even plants—some of them, at least—practice a sort of birth control, as the creosote bush, one of the most characteristic shrubs of the Arizona deserts, certainly does. Instead of permitting every seed to germinate and then to struggle hopelessly for the scanty moisture being captured by already established plants, it disseminates from its roots a growth-inhibiting factor which prevents the germination of any seed too close to a plant already flourishing.

None of this means, of course, that, outside areas set aside
as refuges for nature, we can any longer let her have everywhere her way. All agriculture is an interference with the
state of nature, and as populations increase, they depend for
their existence upon more and more such interference. Once
it was purely local, on so small a scale as hardly to affect the
over-all situation. In what are called the more highly developed countries man's operations come to be more and
more important but, even from his standpoint, terrible mis-
takes have been—still are—made. Overgrazing turned Spain
from a fertile to a semidesert land, and this is believed by
many to have been the ultimate cause of her decline from
prosperity and power to poverty. In much of Arizona south
of the Canyon the ground water is being rapidly exhausted
by the pumps which distribute it over cotton fields, and
much of the region is destined to become more and more
a desert if the present policy is continued.

We have learned more and more effective ways of re-
plenishing with chemicals the soil which otherwise would
have been long ago exhausted and to control with poison
sprays the insects which no longer check one another because the balance between them, their food supply and the
predators, has been upset. To date it can probably be said
that we are winning. But whether in the long run it is
possible for man to create a permanent balance of his own to
take the place of nature's is still an open question. The more
we control, the more control is necessary.

Some years ago a leading economic entomologist ded-

icated a book to a friend "who remarked that insects seem
to be much more prevalent now than thirty years ago, and
suggested that this might be due to the much greater prev-
alence of entomologists." This is something more than a
jest. When we grew crops lusher than any nature had ever
previously known and when we found that a larger and
larger population of insects as well as a larger and larger
population of men could be supported by them, we called
in the entomologist. He gave us the sprays which destroyed
the pests—but unfortunately destroyed at the same time
their enemies, and thus we became increasingly dependent
upon the sprays which had to be made more and more
effective. Even those who are most firmly convinced that
technology will ultimately triumph are ready to admit that
certain pests—notably the mites—are much more destructive now than they once were, because we have killed the
insects which preyed upon them. Whenever you "control"
one aspect of the natural balance, you find to your dismay
that another has got out of hand.

This discussion has wandered far—perhaps farther than it
should—from its starting point, and it is high time to return
to the Canyon where a specific "balance of nature" suggested
the general topic. But the lesson to be learned there does
have its bearing on the lessons which will have to be learned
everywhere, and at least one conclusion can be drawn beyond
the most obvious. In such an area the most benevolent proposal to favor one animal over another should be examined

with the greatest of care, and that conclusion can be extended at least this much farther: wherever a natural or half-natural environment exists—mountain or woodlot or unexploited field—we should not wantonly and blindly interfere drastically with the natural order either because, for instance, we like certain birds better than the hawks that feed upon them or because we begrudge the presence of creatures other than ourselves who occupy a bit of "our" earth or consume a little of its produce. In the long run it will be better for man himself if he can attain to some sympathy with the attitude expressed by Thoreau when moved to disgust by neighbors who would not hesitate to shoot the last pair of hen hawks in town: "I would rather never taste chickens' meat nor hens' eggs than never see a hawk sailing through the upper air again. This sight is worth incomparably more than chicken soup or a boiled egg."

13

Window-shopping

Women have sometimes been known to say that the best part of travel is window-shopping in strange places. A naturalist is sometimes inclined to agree, though he shops in a different window. He, too, goes for a stroll with no particular purpose and no particular destination in view. He is not looking for anything special; only for whatever he has the good luck to find. And like the window-shopper again, he is not planning to take anything material away with him.

Of course you can call this a "nature walk" if you like, but the scornful have succeeded in giving the term certain ridic-

ulous connotations and it is window-shopping that I prefer
to call it. Almost any place where man has not eliminated
every vestige of life other than his own will do and, as a
matter of fact, he has seldom been able to do quite that no
matter how hard he tries.

You might suppose that even germs had been eliminated
from every good hospital, but Charles D. Stewart wrote a
classic essay on a spider he watched while he was confined
to bed. William Beebe wrote a whole book about *Unseen
Life in New York*. And I have heard of one man who made
a study of the mosses he encountered growing between the
bricks of a sidewalk he regularly followed on his way to an
office. Still, some shopping areas are much better than others,
and few are richer than such a relatively unspoiled area as
that around Grand Canyon where the great variety of
environments supports an astonishing variety of plants and
animals.

Shopping districts of the other kind have, so I am told,
become distressingly standardized. There is hardly a city or
even town in the United States where you cannot buy
practically everything that can be found in any other. In
the window of a chain store there are no surprises, and even
the more swanky emporia buy from the same wholesalers no
matter how much "character" they may pretend to have.
Even in foreign lands it is difficult to find a village whose
characteristic products are not displayed here at home, and
I have known more than one female traveler who lugged
something "unique" across the ocean only to find it offered

on her next visit to Macy's. Most goods are by now, like the dandelion, "of cosmopolitan distribution."

But as Thoreau says, "the buckeye does not grow in New England and the mockingbird is rarely heard here." Those who shop for such items can still meet with novelties when they travel. You need a little knowledge—just enough to recognize what you are seeing—and of course the more knowledge you have, the more you will see. But the indispensable minimum is less than the other kind of window-shopper needs if she is to distinguish the original from the commonplace, good bric-a-brac from bad, and "high style" from vulgarization. Some who can do so are amazed that you can tell one butterfly from another, though they remember easily that they saw a better shoe of the same style in some other window six months ago. Names like Paretenodera and Jatropha are no harder to remember than Schiaparelli or Balenciaga. Those who can remember the latter and what they stand for enjoy thoroughly a Sunday stroll which is pure boredom to their reluctant husbands until, perhaps, the husband delays his impatient companion while he inspects the latest cameras, fishing tackle, television set or whatever impinges upon his interests.

For a naturalist who has settled down in some delightful spot, every day is made by some minor discovery or rediscovery. He goes for the same walk time and time again and every time he either sees something new or greets an old friend—animal, vegetable or mineral. Perhaps he finds a flower he has never seen before; he may or may not recognize it as belonging to a familiar genus; he "runs it down" in a *Flora* of the region and he will name it to himself next time. Perhaps he catches a dragonfly at the moment when its gauzy wings are miraculously emerging from the transparent case which inclosed them during the time when the owner was leading an underwater life, or perhaps he sees a praying mantis whipping up with her tail what looks like egg white and will turn out to be, not an angel food cake, but the intricate egg case she alone knows how to make. In each of the five or six "nature books" I have written there has come a time when it was impossible not to quote a certain sentence from Thoreau. And here, inevitably, it suggests itself again: "I had no idea that there was so much going on in Heywood's Meadow." An awful lot always is going on in no matter whose meadow, or forest, or desert.

A well-known entomologist was once asked by a politely curious acquaintance what was the best time and place to look for insects and he replied: "Any time, anyplace." That is probably truer of insects than of any other single organism. But if one is just looking for something that interests a naturalist, it is still true in general, though of course the more one knows, the more likely one is to observe something he knows he does not know.

A distinguished California entomologist, the late T. D. Cockerell, had the coccids (scale insects) as one of his specialties and discovered many new species—one, for instance, when judging a cultivated orchid at a flower show, and another on the Plaza at Vera Cruz while ostensibly engaged in watching the nightly parade of young men and girls passing inspection upon one another. Queens are sometimes less interesting than the little mice under their chairs.

When one sets out to look for some particular thing—a rare plant or animal, for instance—one rarely finds it, at least until after many tries. But one nearly always finds something else just as the Canyon itself was found by a man who had no idea it was there. This is certainly one of the grandest examples of serendipity on record, but minor ones are everyday affairs to enthusiastic window-shoppers. While looking for crossbills on the north rim (and not finding them until days later), I came across two porcupines dozing in a small evergreen and they, sure I must know about their quills, did no more than open one sleepy eye, even when a camera was pushed into their faces. Returning from another expedition, I saw a flock of sixteen half-grown wild turkeys in charge of two adults and probably representing combined families. Botanizing, I was startled to have spring away from under my feet a little red-backed junco whose kind of nest I had never seen and which I could not find now until I had returned time and again to the same spot, flushing the bird each time and finally discovering that she came from under a tuft of coarse grass beneath whose roots was a nest with four blue eggs.

Many professional ornithologists as well as casual "bird watchers" keep "life lists," i.e., a record of all the different species of birds they have seen and identified. Such list-making has the same appeal as any other form of collecting, and though the professionals often smile at themselves, they do it, too. Why botanists, amateur and professional, do not usually do the same I do not know. The appeal is similar and the justification as sound (or as trivial) in the one case as in the other. Serious botanists do, of course, build up herbaria—collections as complete as possible of dried specimens mounted on sheets and filed for reference by family and genus. Such collections are indispensable for certain purely scientific purposes. But they are bulky, cumbersome and, from an aesthetic standpoint, only a little less dismal than animals in formaldehyde. Yet some sort of record is an aid to memory as well as a sort of collection.

My method (which may be commoner than I think) is to note on the margin of Peebles' and Kearney's big *Flora of Arizona* the place and date of every plant I identify for the first time. Some stick in my memory, some do not. But if I fail to remember a flower after I have met it once, I am much more likely to remember it after the second encounter if I am compelled by the record to say, "Sorry, but I have a bad memory for faces" or perhaps, "I remember you, of course, but I have forgot your name." Names are, after all, as important to those interested in plants or animals as they are in cultivating the friendship of human beings. "Hey, you with the bald head and small mouth" is a form of address neither convenient nor polite, and neither is "That rather insignificant blue flower with the fringed petals."

Window-shopping

There are a great many more different plants in most regions than there are birds. Europe has about 450 of the latter, the United States about 650. But in Arizona alone there are more than three thousand kinds of plants. With birds you soon get to the point where there are not many more to be added unless you travel into some unfamiliar world. But a list of plants seen for the first time does not soon come to an end. On my last visit to the north rim I did add one new bird which I had somehow never happened to see before. But even on my own home ground any little jaunt between February and November is pretty sure to decorate the margin of the *Flora* with one or two new notations. And at least some flowers can be found blooming in every month of the year.

A fairly recently revised edition of Asa Gray's long standard *Manual of Botany* gives only a little more than four thousand species for an area covering most of the eastern section of the United States—West as far as the western boundary of Minnesota and southward as far as the southern boundary of Virginia. That this number is only a third larger than the number to be found in Arizona alone is due to the fact that the immense variety of altitudes and climates in Arizona provides suitable conditions for an immense variety of different plants. And since there is more than six thousand feet difference between the bottom of Grand Canyon and the highest point on its rim, one might expect to find a considerable proportion of all the plants known to grow anywhere in Arizona within that six thousand vertical feet, which corresponds to something like 3,500 miles difference in latitude at sea level.

Though no complete check list for the park area has been compiled, even the casual visitor will notice how rapidly and frequently he passes from one floral region to another, and competent opinion is that a very large proportion of all the plants found anywhere in the state grow somewhere in the Canyon. Less expected and perhaps even more striking is the fact that there are a few which were for long known *only* there. For such rarities any assiduous window-shopper will certainly look. What is probably the most interesting I did indeed find—when I wasn't looking for it.

Not far from Cape Royal a little wet-weather stream called Clear Creek has cut one of the innumerable side canyons which lead their waters ultimately to the Colorado here flowing nearly eight thousand feet below. If you scramble down its right side, you will come soon upon a tiny shelter made long ago by some Indian who built masonry walls to enclose the space under an overhanging rock. One would take it for a mere storage bin, but the archeologists say it shows unmistakable signs of actual habitation —how long ago and whether by more than a single solitary hunter no one, I think, can more than guess.

Pass by this reminder of a time when solitude was not something one had to look for even in Grand Canyon, and you will come suddenly upon a beautiful and surprising spot. The Canyon widens suddenly, and for several hundred feet along a sheer wall of red sandstone runs a ledge ten or twelve feet wide and overhung for part of that distance by the cliff wall. This is precisely the sort of shallow cave the cliff dwellers frequently chose, but there are no signs that any pueblo was ever built here. At one point a steady drip of water from the stone wall forms a shallow pool on the ledge and trickles away over the end to join Clear Creek. All this —the warm exposure, the overhanging roof and the abundant moisture—create over an area of a few hundred square feet a striking example of what the ecologists call a "microclimate." Various types of vegetation flourish—including yellow columbine which one would not be likely to find in many places even high on the Canyon wall. And from many damp little crevices in the cliff wall comes trailing down the stems of a sort of hanging-basket plant covered with small bright yellow flowers. It is flourishing exuberantly under just the conditions it prefers.

This plant was one I had never seen before and in some mysterious way looked as though it was unusual. I picked a few blossoms and leaves and when I ran it down through the key of my *Flora* I discovered that my hunch had been right. The plant was *Potentillia osterhoutii*. No wonder the flowers look a good deal like those of the wild strawberry since the genera are loosely related members of the rose family. But "known only from the Grand Canyon," said my authority.

I am a little sorry to have to report that since this last statement was made *Potentillia osterhoutii* has been found in a few other places. But it is still an unusual plant and it raises the question which such organisms with a very limited distribution always raise. Are they recent creations of the evolutionary process and just getting a start, or are they part of what botanists call a "relic flora"—the last lingering members of a disappearing species managing to survive in a few localities just as certain still living birds and beasts also do? Will *osterhoutii* be common some thousands of years hence or will it disappear like that mere film of Moenkopi conglomerate still clinging to parts of the South Rim?

Perhaps the most famous case of a relic-plant rescued just at the point of final extinction is the fairly common flowering shrub of the garden, *Franklinia altamaha*. It was found by John Bartram growing wild near the Altamaha River in Georgia and put into cultivation. But since 1790 it has never been found in the wild again. When specimens of such presumably relic-plants are found in two widely separated localities, the puzzle is even stranger. Consider, for example, the small fern with a long name, *Ceterach dalhousiae*. It looks rather like a spleenwort but unlike most ferns it grows in very arid regions. In the United States it is found only in the mountains of two contiguous southern Arizona counties. Elsewhere it is known only from Abyssinia and the mountains of southern Asia. Does this mean that it was once of world-wide distribution, and if so why does it now survive only locally in areas scattered over three continents?

Relatively few people have ever seen *Potentillia oster-*

Window-shopping

houtii; fewer still have recognized it or would have been interested if they had. But it is a new item in my collection, something to be brought back from a window-shopping expedition. It is also something more, because it raises the whole question of rare and disappearing organisms. Since one of its few footholds happens to be in a national park, its chances of survival are better than those of most unusual animals and plants. Many others more spectacular will disappear, many of them all but unnoticed, as fewer and fewer of even the crannies and corners of this earth escape "utilization" and "improvement."

"No great loss," so the majority will certainly say. Perhaps they are right so far as any individual plant or animal is concerned. But cumulatively it means the gradual reduction of that seemingly almost infinite profusion and variety which nature created.

Until exploration opened up new worlds a few centuries ago, no one had any idea how great this profusion and variety was. It stunned the imagination of naturalists and of many laymen besides. The desire to know it better or even just to see more of it for oneself gave Europe innumerable books, collections and gardens. Since that time the exploiters who followed the explorers have been busy both at home and abroad rooting up, exterminating or merely pushing to the wall species after species in order to make room for themselves and for "useful" products. The variety of nature grows less and less. The monotony of the chain store begins to dominate more and more completely. One must go farther and farther to find a window in which anything not found elsewhere is to be seen.

More than a hundred species and subspecies of mammals are known to have disappeared from the face of the earth since the beginning of the Christian era. Along with them have gone perhaps as many birds and an unknown number of humbler creatures. How many plants have suffered extinction has not, so far as I am aware, been even guessed at. But the list must be a long one.

A few of us—but probably only a few—put upon every unique kind of living thing what most would call a "sentimental" or, at most, a "mystical value." We see in the death of a species the most startlingly ultimate, irrevocable and irretrievable of natural phenomena. Individuals usually have descendants like themselves and in a sense they live on. But the death of a species is death in a more absolute sense. What dies then is the whole possibility of life in one of its forms, and the universe is the poorer for something it will never possess again.

There is no work of art so precious that it might not conceivably be reconstructed. But whatever living thing dies as a species is irrecoverable, and neither Shakespeare nor Michelangelo is so dead as the dodo. Even in the middle of total war we make some show of attempting to avoid the destruction of irreplaceable works of art. A Madonna by a minor Renaissance painter is, we say, "irreplaceable." But more and more local authorities in country as well as town spray roadsides with "weed killers," indifferent to the fact that roadsides are among the last refuges of many native plants.

As usual, that best of all window-shoppers, Henry Thoreau, put the feelings of a minority better than they will ever be able to put it for themselves: "I spend a considerable portion of my time observing the habits of the wild animals, my brute neighbors. By their various movements and migrations they fetch the year about me. . . . But when I consider that the nobler animals have been exterminated here—the cougar, panther, lynx, wolverine, bear, moose, deer, the beaver, the turkey, etc., etc.,—I cannot but feel as if I lived in a tamed and, as it were, emasculated country. Would not the motions of these larger and wilder animals have been more significant still? Is it not a maimed and imperfect nature that I am conversant with? As if I were to study a tribe of Indians that had lost all its warriors. Do not the forest and the meadow now lack expression, now that I never see nor think of the moose with a lesser forest on his head in the one nor of the beaver in the other? When I think what were the various sounds and notes, the migrations and works, and changes of fur and plumage which ushered in the spring and marked the other seasons of the year, I am reminded that this my life in nature, this particular round of natural phenomena which I call a year, is lamentably incomplete. I listen to a concert in which many parts are wanting. The whole civilized country is to some extent turned into a city, and I am that citizen whom

I pity. . . . Primitive Nature is most interesting to me. I take infinite pains to know all the phenomena of spring, for instance, thinking that I have here the entire poem, and then, to my chagrin, I hear that it is but an imperfect copy that I possess and have read, that my ancestors have torn out many of the first leaves and grandest passages, and mutilated it in many places. I should not like to think that some demi-god had come before me and picked out some of the best of the stars. I wish to know an entire heaven and an entire earth."

Since Thoreau's time more pages have been torn from his New England and more of its grandest passages mutilated. The loons, for instance, came regularly to Walden Pond and inspired him to write one of his most charming passages. Even then, however: "At rumor of his arrival all the Mill-dam sportsmen are on the alert, in gigs and on foot, two by two and three by three, with patent rifles and conical balls and spy-glasses. They come rustling through the woods like autumn leaves, at least ten men to one loon." Today, so Roger Tory Peterson reports, "It flies over Concord in migration, but very rarely alights."

I doubt that loons are so often shot at by "sportsmen" as they were in Thoreau's time. But "progress" is a perhaps deadlier enemy of nature than the hunter ever was. At this moment, so I learn from the press, Walden Pond is being improved into a bathing beach and, in all probability, tank trucks are spraying roadsides from which will be eliminated the humble little flowers Thoreau loved. One must now go to a national park to find a nature not more drastically expurgated than Concord was in his day. From Grand Canyon itself the cougar and the wolf have been all but exterminated in the name of what we call "predator control" and Thoreau called "depriving a tribe of its warriors." Much—very much—is still left, though everywhere outside (and sometimes within) the legally protected areas destruction goes on. "The squirrel has leaped to another tree; the hawk has circled further off, and has now settled upon a new eyrie; but the woodman is preparing to lay his axe at the root of that also."

Such thoughts as these are, I am glad to say, afterthoughts. While window-shopping in a region as rich as Grand Canyon still is, I am too constantly diverted by what I see to think much of what is no longer to be found or of the fact that for succeeding generations my diversion will be less rewarding than it is now. If a porcupine is an event —they are protected in the park itself but cruelly left to die in traps within the forest just outside—there are so many minor items that I must pass some of them by.

Of course none of this is science or likely to add anything to it. The "serious amateur" still occasionally adds his bit, but the day is long past when the mere window-shopper has one chance in a thousand of seeing anything not seen and duly noted long before. To pick up even what Newton called "a smoother pebble or a prettier shell than ordinary, whilst the great ocean of truth lay all undiscovered before me" one usually needs nowadays to be a specialist, and even within the limits of one science the specialist must specialize. He is a zoologist or a botanist or a cytologist or a biochemist and if he is a botanist he limits himself to the ferns or the fungi, the grasses or the flowering plants; and even then he may be regarded by the real specialists as inclined to spread himself rather thin.

Once when I was window-shopping in a side canyon of the Catalina Mountains I met a stranger who turned out to be the greatest living authority on the ants of the United States. Noticing my binoculars he amiably told me that he had seen some interesting-looking birds not far away. "What were they?" "Oh, I don't know the names of any birds. In fact I try not to know any. There are so many ants that it is all I can do to remember them."

Many specialists are very contemptuous of such activities as mine—but not all of them are. Some steal time from their exacting pursuits to be amateurs at something else or even, like me, of things in general. Thus they recapture some of the spirit of the old naturalists who, whether they were professionals like Linnaeus or hobbyists like Gilbert White, lived at a time when there seemed nothing absurd about taking all nature as one's province. And there are even some, eminent in their specialty, who experience a certain nostalgia for the days when the burden of accumulated knowledge was less heavy. "The road," said Cervantes, "is always better than the inn" and discovering is more fun that catching up with what has been discovered.

Window-shopping

N. J. Berrill, the McGill zoologist, puzzles over one aspect of the problem when he complains that the beginning student of today is middle-aged and past the years when his mind should be most adventurously active before he has mastered enough of what is already known of his subject to attempt any contributions to it. The late William Morton Wheeler, one of the most competent of specialists in a highly specialized field, spoke closer to my own condition when he wrote, not only sympathetically but even enviously, of those who like me have assumed no responsibility:

> Our intellects will never be equal to exhausting biological reality. Why animals and plants are as they are, we shall never know; of how they have come to be what they are, our knowledge will always be extremely fragmentary, because we are dealing only with the recent phases of an immense and complicated history, most of the records of which are lost beyond all chance of recovery; but that organisms are as they are, that apart from the members of our own species, they are our only companions in an infinite and unsympathetic waste of electrons, planets, nebulae and suns, is a perennial joy and consolation. We should all be happier if we were less completely obsessed by problems and somewhat more accessible to the aesthetic and emotional appeal of our materials, and it is doubtful whether, in the end, the growth of biological science would be appreciably retarded. It quite saddens me to think that when I cross the Styx, I may find myself among so many professional biologists, condemned to keep on trying to solve problems, and that Pluto, or whoever is in charge down there now, may condemn me to sit

forever trying to identify specimens from my own specific and generic diagnoses, while the amateur entomologists, who have not been damned professors, are permitted to roam at will among the fragrant asphodels of the Elysian meadows, netting gorgeous, ghostly butterflies until the end of time.

When the young John Muir had reached the Cumberland Mountains in the course of his "Thousand Mile Walk to the Gulf" (exclusively a window-shopping expedition), he spent the night with a serious blacksmith struggling to survive in the remote backwoods of a region lately devastated by the Civil War. When he was asked what had brought him and replied that he had come to look for plants this dialogue ensued:

"What kind of plants?"
"Oh, all kinds; grass, weeds, flowers, trees, mosses, ferns—almost everything that grows is interesting to me. . . ."
"You look like a strong-minded man," he replied, "and surely you are able to do something better than wander over the country and look at weeds and blossoms. These are hard times, and real work is required of every man that is able. Picking up blossoms doesn't seem to be a man's work at all in any kind of times."
To this I replied, "You are a believer in the Bible, are you not?" "Oh, yes." "Well, you know that Solomon was a strong-minded man and he is generally believed to have been the very wisest man the world ever saw, and yet he considered it was worth while to study plants; not only to go and pick them as I am doing, but to study them; and you know that

we are told that he wrote a book about plants, not only the great Cedars of Lebanon, but of little bits of things growing in the cracks of the walls.

"Therefore you see that Solomon differed very much more from you than from me in this matter. I'll warrant you he had many a long ramble in the mountains of Judaea, and had he been a Yankee he would likely have visited every weed in the land. And again, do you not remember that Christ told his disciples to 'consider the lilies how they grow,' and compared their beauty with Solomon in all his glory? Now whose advice am I to take, yours or Christ's? Christ says 'Consider the lilies.' You say 'Don't consider them. It isn't worth while for any strong-minded man.' "

According to Muir the honest blacksmith was silenced and apparently convinced. To any window-shoppers who feel themselves "strong-minded men" and truant from more justifiable occupation I recommend that they follow Muir's argument back to its probably unrecognized source in the thought of the seventeenth and eighteenth centuries when the great age of natural history was opening. Muir may have been a bit sportive in citing his Biblical examples, but his predecessors were not. Nature, so they thought, was what Sir Thomas Browne had called it, "the art of God." To consider the lilies was to consider His work and therefore an act of worship. Not to consider them was to be contemptuously indifferent toward what He had created for man's admiration. And not even the humblest living thing failed to declare His glory since, as an ancient patriotic writer had said, "He

created in heaven the angels and in the earth, worms; nor
was He superior in the one case or inferior in the other. If no
other hands but His could create the angels, neither could
any other create the worms."

When the young Thoreau proclaimed in his graduation address that "this curious world which we inhabit is more wonderful than it is convenient; more beautiful than it is useful
. . . more to be admired and enjoyed than used," he was
saying precisely what the modern world most emphatically
does not believe. But like Muir he was consciously or un-
consciously echoing what had once been the premise of the
old naturalists who were less intent upon "useful knowledge"
than upon the discovery of what John Ray, England's first
great naturalist, was to call "The Wisdom of God Manifest
in the Works of the Creation." "Let us then," he wrote, "consider the Works of God and observe the operations of his
hands. . . . No creature in the sublunary world is capable
of so doing, besides man, and yet we are deficient herein."

Linnaeus, who corresponded with Ray, reflected the same
attitudes and when he boasts that no man has had the privilege of seeing more examples of the variety of nature's creations, he is speaking not only of a privilege but also of an
obligation discharged.

How trivial, then, should we hold window-shopping to be?
Perhaps it all depends upon whose windows we shop in.

14

What men? What needs?

Many beautiful areas in many parts of the Southwest are far less accessible and far less frequented than Grand Canyon. Some of them I have visited again and again during the course of twenty years but never without seeing some evidence of human activity which had diminished or destroyed things I had come to enjoy. Something precious had disappeared because it could not coexist with energetic exploitation.

"Oh, well," I have sometimes said to myself, "most of it will probably outlast my time." But I have never been completely comforted by the thought. All concern for posterity aside, I do not like to think that something I have loved may cease to be, even when I am no longer here to take my joy of it.

Perhaps no radical and permanent solution of the problem is possible. The world grows more crowded year by year and at an ever increasing rate. Men push farther and farther in their search for "resources" to be exploited, even for more mere space to occupy. Increasingly they tend to think of the terrestrial globe as *their* earth. They never doubt their right to deal with it as they think fit—and what they think fit usually involves the destruction of what nature has thought fit during many millions of years.

Only the United States among highly developed nations can still offer its citizens the opportunity to visit large regions where nature still dominates the scene. And that is because only the United States began at a sufficiently early stage of its development to set aside as public lands some of the most attractive of such regions. We had national parks before England had established so much as one small nature reserve. In so far as this is true it suggests hope. We have not been entirely blind to what we have, nor to the danger of losing it.

"Never have I seen such wonders or met landlords so worthy of their land. They have, and still have, the power to ravage it; and instead they have made it a garden." Thus wrote the visiting English naturalist, James Fisher, in the book called *Wild America* upon which he and Roger Tory

What men? What needs?

Peterson collaborated. Nor is the tribute wholly undeserved. But Mr. Fisher politely refrained from stressing either the unearned blessing we received when we inherited the continent from a red man too little advanced technologically to have defaced it, or the fact that the "power to ravage" which the National Parks Act was intended to hold forever in check still ominously exists. How much longer the check will hold is uncertain; and there are signs that the American people—or at least its leaders—are less concerned than was the generation of Theodore Roosevelt to preserve for posterity some of the wild portions of our heritage.

No one opposes "conservation" as such. But many insist upon defining it in their own way. There are always rival claims to every unexploited area, and even the parks cannot stand up against such claims unless the strength of their own claim is recognized. Unless we think of intangible values as no less important than material resources, unless we are willing to say that man's need of and right to what the parks and wildernesses provide are as fundamental as any of his material needs, they are lost.

Those who would cut the timber, slaughter the animals as game, turn cattle loose to graze, flood the area with dams, or even open them up to real estate subdivision are fond of saying, "After all, human needs come first." But of what needs and of what human beings are we thinking? Of the material needs (or rather profits) of a few ranchers and lumbermen, or of the mental and physical health, the education and spiritual experiences, of a whole population? We do not tear down a high school because the building industry can prove that it could profitably erect an apartment house on the site and that tenants would be glad to occupy it. We say, instead, that education pays off in a different way and that the space occupied by schools is not wasted. Much the same thing we say also of the space taken up by the green of a city square. But if parks and other public lands are to be held only until someone can show that a "use" has been found for them, they will not last very much longer. If we recognize that there is more than one kind of utility and that the parks are, at the present moment, being put to the best use to be found for them, then they may last a long time—until, perhaps, overpopulation has reached the point where the struggle for mere animal survival is so brutal that no school or theater, no concert hall or church, can be permitted to "waste" the land on which it stands.

No other recent threat is quite so fantastic as that recently raised in Arizona where a small group of farmers cultivating the irrigated desert have persuaded a small group of ranchers to adopt with them the highly unorthodox notion that the forests clothing the watersheds are "wasting" water which might be used for cotton or other crops.

Both ancient and modern history provide many examples of countrysides, even of whole nations, destroyed by the destruction of their forests. So far as I am aware, there is no known case where the stripping of mountains had any beneficial effect. Yet a picked group of experts was employed to report on the proposal; it issued a rather careful report—sponsored jointly by the Salt River Valley Water Users Association and the University of Arizona—which boils down to the statement that the deforestation of certain mountain ranges in northeastern Arizona *might* provide more water behind the dams. Then the interested groups distributed a so-called summary of the report in which the "mights" and other qualifications are largely removed and they enlisted the support of the governor of the state as well as of at least one of the largest banks.

Here are some of the highlights from one of the principal speakers at a meeting called by the proponents of the scheme: "Outside of agriculture, there's more confusion, more ignorance and more self-interest concerning the conservation movement than there is about almost any other important movement in the country. . . . We should forget about soil erosion as the banner of conservation. . . . I have just written off the forests of the Southwest and a large part of those located elsewhere in the United States. . . . No longer will millions of trees keep a large percentage of rain and snowfall from reaching the ground. . . . We need chemical sprays that will destroy trees and brush at low cost. . . . As this [public] land's productiveness is increased, I believe it should pass into the hands of private owners. . . . Private ownership of land is the basis of our democratic society. . . . Conservation is an economic problem. If we could amputate sentimentalism, romanticism and hobbyism from the body of conservation, progress would be faster and more certain than it is."

The official summary of the original report gives a more detailed picture both of what the plan proposes and of the kind of earth it envisages. "The program . . . includes drastic thinning of ponderosa pine stands. . . . The pulp industry will not develop fast enough to provide wholesale cleanup of all forested areas. . . . As an adjunct to a treatment program, a speed-up in the harvesting of timber on the watershed is indicated. . . . It is not beyond reasonable expectation that the cities of central Arizona will someday have to cover with plastic or other impervious material an area that will furnish those cities the highest quality of soft water."

Yet the forests this group proposes to destroy are not private property nor even state property. They belong to the national government and therefore to all the people. But only, so it was assumed, this particular group has any real right to them because only its members propose to make a monetary profit. One of the most important newspapers in the state supports their claim in an editorial relying upon the premise that "human needs come first" without asking, as we have insisted upon asking, "What needs?" and "What human beings?"

The assumed answer is obviously "Only the 'needs' of a small group of men producing surplus commodities." Because these men hope to make a quick profit by disregarding, among so many other things, "soil conservation" and by

What men? What needs?

destroying a national forest, they think they have the right, not only to seize public lands for a very dangerous and unpromising experiment, but also to deprive everybody else, including generations yet to come, of the benefits their government had assured them. Who needs surplus cotton as much as thousands of today (and millions of tomorrow) need space, fresh air, and a chance to see what a forest looks like?

Perhaps this monstrous proposal to adopt deforestation as a technique of "conservation" will be defeated by its inherent preposterousness rather than by a proper answer to the questions "What men?" and "What needs?" Yet in the end they will still be the crucial questions, and the answers we give will determine, not only the fate of all our "resources," but also what such parks as we may be able to save will themselves become.

Just what needs of just what men should these parks and other natural areas serve? How natural should a "natural" area be kept? How much should it be "developed" when every development or "improvement" makes it just that much less natural and unspoiled?

Consider, for example, the question of "accessibility." An area that cannot be reached is obviously not being put to use. On the other hand, one reached too easily becomes a mere "resort" to which people flock for purposes just as well served by golf courses, swimming pools, and summer hotels. Parks are often described as "recreation areas" and so they are. But the term "recreation" as ordinarily used does not imply much stress upon the kind of experience which Grand Canyon, despite the flood of visitors that comes to it, still does provide—namely, the experience of being in the presences of nature's ways and nature's work.

Proponents of the recently defeated proposal to flood the Dinosaur Canyon by building a great water-storage dam answered defenders of the national monument within which it lies by saying that the "recreational value" would be increased rather than diminished. They were so sure of their case that they showed pictures of the gaunt canyon with the bones of prehistoric monsters exposed *in situ* and contrasted them with other pictures of artificial lakes behind other dams where bathing girls reclined on sand beaches and speedboats cut across the waters. From their own point of view they were right. But however delightful bathing girls and speedboats may be, they are at least different from, rather than merely better than, what Grand or Dinosaur Canyon provides. Moreover, the places where one may find bathing girls and speedboats are multiplying, while those where one may find solitude, quiet, and the grand spectacles of nature become fewer and fewer.

What is called progress is too often the exchange of one thing (good or bad) for something else, good or bad. Even education means too often learning something at the cost of forgetting something else. But both are pursued so uncritically that we seldom stop to ask whether what we get and learn is worth what we are losing and forgetting.

What men? What needs?

A majority, increasing perhaps, is ready to settle for "recreation" in this most recent sense, and many may by now actually prefer it. This is so much the age of technology and the machine that machines come to be loved for their own sake rather than used for other ends. Instead, for instance, of valuing the automobile because it may take one to a national park, the park comes to be valued because it is a place the automobile may be used to reach. A considerable number of automobilists would like when they get there to do what they do at home or at the country club. An even greater number prefers to drive straight through so that they can use their machine to get somewhere else. They feel that to stop is simply to waste time, because time spent without the employment of some gadget is time wasted—though it may to some extent be salvaged by turning on the radio. But is it for such as these that the parks should be maintained?

We, reply the proponents of developing further "the recreational facilities" of the national parks, live in a democracy, and the majority should rule. It is purely a question of the greatest good for the greatest number. But they forget to ask what if "the greatest good" and "for the greatest number" do not coincide? Suppose that the greatest number does want the kind of recreation to be had in so many other places and that only a smaller number wants something increasingly hard to find. Would the greater good of the smaller number justify the reservation of certain areas for them?

Granted that the greatness of a good is, unlike the greatness of a number, susceptible of only subjective estimation, we still do recognize to some slight extent the justice of reserving a limited number of airwave channels for the "educational" and "cultural" programs which the greatest number most certainly does not prefer to comedians and jazz. Of certain other "minority rights" we hear a great deal. But are all such rights exclusively political, religious and racial? Are not the intellectual, aesthetic and emotional rights of a minority just as sacred? Does democracy demand that they be disregarded?

The best possible compromise in the case of parks and other public lands is to recognize that they are competed for by both the exploiters to whom an absolute "No" must be said and by the seekers after "recreation" who have certain legitimate but not exclusive claims. To those with different "needs" should be allotted a reasonable share. That does not mean a share in each individual area, because to attempt to give that would inevitably be to destroy completely the share of the minority. It can only mean a distinction between some nationally administered areas which are primarily for "recreation" and others which preserve in a recognizable state something of nature herself.

The wilderness area, the protected nature reserve, and the recreation resort are different things: the first is for the smallest minority—that which is physically and psychologically up to the strenuousness of really primitive living. The second is for the larger minority which is interested in wild animals, in plant life, and in natural scenery, even though unprepared for life in a real wilderness. The third, of course, is for the majority whose tastes are not essentially different from those who frequent commercial resorts.

The increasing size and increasing mobility of our population makes it inevitable that the more sedate "nature lover" should favor whatever will facilitate his pushing into the wilderness area, and the seeker after mere recreation whatever would make the nature reserve more attractive to him. If the desires of either are too eagerly met, the ultimate result will be that only "resorts" can continue long to exist. But if the desirability of the distinctions is recognized, it is not difficult to maintain them. It is, indeed, largely a matter of easy accessibility and "modern facilities."

We have come to assume that "good roads" are, anywhere and everywhere, an absolute good and an unmixed blessing. Few if any other expenditures of public money are so generally approved as those for road building. Congress (and the public which elects it) can always be expected to hesitate longer over an appropriation to acquire or protect a national park than over one to build a highway into it. Yet there is nothing which so rapidly turns a wilderness into a reserve and a reserve into a resort. An astonishing number of those for whom a national park (or any other region commonly regarded as "worth seeing") is primarily an excuse for exercising their automobile will turn aside from even ten miles of a good unpaved road and take instead a four-lane highway, no matter where it leads. It is not unreasonable to protect both wilderness areas and nature reserves by keeping them for those who are willing to take a certain amount of trouble to get there.

Those who favor better roads and various other enticements are no doubt honest in their professed desire to promote what they call "fuller use" of the wildernesses and the parks. But what they are encouraging is not a fuller but a different use—incompatible with the original one. It would hardly be practicable to examine every visitor to wilderness or reserve and to make him prove that he has come for a legitimate purpose. But it is perfectly possible to make the test automatically by having the road ask the question: "Are you willing to take a little trouble to get there?" Though the proposal to prepare deliberately for such automatic questioning will seem fantastic to many, that is only because ours is an age—the very first, perhaps—which has come to assume that "the most accessible" is always "the best"—in education, art and entertainment as well as in recreation.

Up until now the original purposes of the national parks and monuments has been fairly well preserved—partly as the result of a more or less conscious policy, more perhaps because limitations of money and time have slowed down the tendency to pervert them. Now that the integrity of the parks is being increasingly threatened by would-be exploiters as well as by the simple pressure of an increasing population looking for "recreation," a definite policy of protection from both ought to be formulated. Along with the question

What men? What needs?

of "good roads," especially within the parks themselves, it would have to judge all the other "improvements" and "facilities" proposed and sometimes provided.

Grand Canyon is still what it should be: one of the most accessible of the nature reserves. Merely as a spectacle it is popularly recognized as one of the "wonders of the world" and could not reasonably be denied even to those who desire no more than to look at it and go away, satisfied that another item on the list has been checked off. Yet despite the tremendous number of visitors, the inaccessibility of all but a very limited part has prevented it from being spoiled as Yellowstone has been—to the extent that at Yellowstone one is reminded of man and his works at least as often as of nature's.

At the Canyon most of the visitors willingly confine themselves to a very restricted area, and if that area is by now almost a mere resort, there is a great deal left that is not. Diminishing accessibility acts as a very effective filter. Some (but not too many) make the little effort necessary to seek out the still lonely nearby portions of the rim where one may be alone with nature and one's thoughts. Fewer make the journey to the bottom. Fewer still—probably not so many as visit even the remoter of our wilderness areas—risk the considerable adventure any departure from the established trails involves. Plainly visible from the most frequented section of the rim are canyons and buttes which, so far as we know, no human foot has ever trod. There must be few other easily accessible places on earth where it is possible to look into areas never actually explored by man.

That all of this should still be true is due in part to the simple fact that the scale and ruggedness of the Canyon has made it very difficult to assimilate it into the routines of modern man. But it is due in part also to deliberate intention. First-class roads lead into the park and for a few miles along the south rim beyond the hotels and village. They stop there, and all the "facilities" have been confined to an even smaller area. Those who insist upon driving cars, listening to their radios, or writing post cards and are loath to get too far from conventional beds or restaurant food do not need any prohibition to keep them where they should be. Their own tastes are sufficiently eloquent persuaders. Thus the Grand Canyon National Park as it now stands and is now administered represents what is probably the best possible compromise between the desires and needs of the different classes of people who visit it and the limitations which have to be imposed if it is not to degenerate into a resort differing from other resorts only in being provided with a different backdrop. Even the fact that the north rim is less accessible to the most densely populated parts of the nation has made it less visited and, for that reason, it is even more conspicuously still a "natural" area.

Occasionally one hears some theoretical objection to the monopoly of the whole hotel-autocourt-restaurant system which on the south rim is held by the Fred Harvey Company and on the north rim by the Union Pacific's Utah

What men? What needs?

Parks Company. But whatever unfortunate aspects monopoly management can develop, those who compare the situation within the parks with that prevailing in much visited
areas outside them are likely to conclude that a properly
controlled monopolistic concession is easier to manage than
free competition which seems everywhere to encourage
blatant advertising, confusion, noise, and the whole ugly
paraphernalia involved when the vulgarest whims of the tourist are catered to. Monopoly has no need of neon signs and
loud-speakers. Neither does it, at the Canyon at least, set
up county-fair attractions to compete with the exhibits and
with the interpretive talks the Park Service itself provides.
Like the Park Administration, the Harvey Company, especially, seems to have reached a very acceptable compromise between what floods of visitors must have and what
would destroy the uniqueness of the region they have come
to enjoy.

What would soon happen to the park as a whole were it
in private hands is all too clearly suggested by what has happened in a little enclave lying a few miles west of the tourist
center on the south rim. It exists because in 1903, before this
or any other national park existed, one Daniel Hogan staked
out there a claim to a copper mine and had it signed by
Theodore Roosevelt himself. The mine proved worthless so
far as copper was concerned, but the claim passed to other
hands and in 1953 uranium ore—said to be of the highest
grade known on the American continent—was discovered.
Today it is being actively mined and on the privately owned

patch at the rim a minor tourist "attraction" has been built.

Suppose other rich mines should be discovered and suppose (what is hard *not* to suppose) the whole park should be opened to prospectors under the plea of "national necessity." The clank of cable cars would banish the great silence of the Canyon, and innumerable Tasty Tepees would spring up around them.

Even assuming that no such deliberate exploitation and spoilation should take place, there is still the question of how long the present successful compromises of the Park Service can last. They cannot be expected to maintain themselves; they represent a compromise that is happy to date but unstable nevertheless. Notoriously there exist within the Park Service itself differences of opinion between "the developers" and "the preservers." Regularly, a certain number of visitors look sourly at the mule trains setting out for the Canyon bottom. Mules they regard as disgraceful anachronisms in an age of technological triumphs. "Why don't you build a funicular railway?" they ask. "Or even a series of skilifts?"

Fortunately, either enterprise would be considerably more difficult than any who have not made a trip to the bottom can realize. But suppose that either were undertaken. It would not mean that a greater number would enjoy what the lesser number now enjoy, only that they would enjoy something different and something more like what is obtainable elsewhere. That the Canyon is not "conquered" is one of the most impressive things about it.

Most of our wildernesses not exploited out of existence are no doubt destined to become parks in time. Are the parks in turn doomed to become mere resorts? Ultimately perhaps. How rapidly will depend largely upon the philosophy which the Park Service formulates and the support it can win for it.

How much difference will it make whether it does or doesn't? How many people care or should care?

To all such questions the answer depends upon what one believes about the nature of man, about his desires and his needs, above all about the permanence and unique importance of certain among them.

If desire for contact with nature and some sense of unity and sympathy with her are merely vestigial hankerings surviving from the time when man lived in a more primitive culture; if these vestiges can, and should, fade gradually away as he becomes more and more completely adapted to a civilization founded upon technology rather than the natural processes—then obviously there is not much point in trying to preserve opportunities for gratifying the hankering. If what wildernesses and national parks supply is merely a kind of "recreation" for which more easily supplied kinds are equally useful and pleasant, then they are indeed merely extravagantly inefficient methods of providing it. If, in

other words, interest and delight in nature are mere anachronisms, perhaps they should be discouraged rather than
gratified, and the effort spent upon them devoted to weaning
mankind away.

Many practical planners and many social philosophers—
also, perhaps, the majority of unthinking men—go upon the
more or less unqualified assumption that such is indeed the
case. Robert Moses, who has done so much to mitigate
the gauntness of concrete and steel in the New York area, has
sometimes been accused of accepting too readily the park-
way and the city park as substitutes for anything remotely
suggesting the natural. And his reply is: "A lot of people
. . . hate the country and love congestion. It's all very well
to say, 'Who wants to live in Brooklyn?'—but the answer is,
three million people do, and just try to move any of them."

So far as the facts go, Mr. Moses is undoubtedly right.
Many people—whether you call them adjusted to or corrupted by the conditions under which they have lived—prefer "God's concrete," which actually is more characteristic
of the God they worship. Even if, dutifully rather than gladly,
they "go away for a vacation," they prefer it to be at some
highly artificial resort. Even at Grand Canyon they would
complain that there isn't anything to *do* and nothing to be
seen that you can't see in ten minutes.

Some of the more philosophically inclined, including some
critics of literature and the arts, say something like this:
"Ours is the age of man, machines and useful knowledge.
We are no longer part of nature either physically or emo-

What men? What needs?

tionally. To the relatively slight degree that we are still dependent upon natural products, we have learned how to manage their production with maximum efficiency and there is no reason why we should let nature take her course about anything. Animals, other than domestic and game, are good for nothing except for what we can learn by dissecting or by experimenting upon them. All this fuss about saving the parks is merely a sentimental plea for wasting ground that could be grazed and lumber that could be cut. Millions today rarely see anything except concrete and steel and don't know what to make of anything else if they do happen to see it. Their proportionate numbers are bound to increase. Cities are healthier and more convenient anyway, and any regret over man's increasing self-sufficiency is merely what a certain well-known Columbia University professor used to call 'nostalgia for a lower form of civilization.' "

If you prefer to put it even more abstractly and in the grotesque new terms which abstraction calls upon, consider the remarks of the ecologist, I. Vernadsky, who proposed in the technical journal, *American Science* (1945), the new word "noosphere" to contrast with the term "biosphere" which ecologists—regrettably perhaps—are already accustomed to use. The biosphere is simply the earth as the processes, balances, and conflicts of nature make it; the "noosphere" is those portions of the earth where whatever conditions exist do so because man has imposed his will rather than nature's upon them. Civilization, according to this notion, is the process by which the noosphere destroys and re-places the biosphere, and it will be complete when no bio-sphere any longer exists. That, in philosophical language (or jargon), would represent the final achievement of that "con-quest of nature" of which we boast so much.

As population grows, the biosphere inevitably shrinks, and for even the few who would like to live in a world where nature is very conspicuously present, it becomes harder and harder to do so—as even the suburbanite realizes while his suburb grows and "prospers." The Texan, J. Frank Dobie once wrote: "Many times I have thought that the greatest happiness possible to a man—probably not to a woman—is to become civilized, to know the pageant of the past, to love the beautiful, to have just ideas of values and proportions, and then, retaining his animal spirits and appetites, to live in a wilderness where nature is congenial, with a few bar-barisms to afford picturesqueness and human relations. . . . According to this ideal civilization is necessary to give man a perspective; but is otherwise either a mere substitute for primitiveness or else a background to flee from." And then he adds: "Such [an ideal] was never practicable except to a few individuals who in retreating from society substituted camp fires for ivory towers. In this shrinking world it becomes less and less practicable. It precludes the idea of a civilized democracy—though any democracy will be tolerant of non-conformists who draw off to one side as well as of those who march with the ranks."

What men? What needs?

The concession made in that last clause is a large one. Ivory towers (including those centered around a campfire) have often been more than things to shut oneself up in—they have been also towers to look out from, and places to think new thoughts or to remember old ones. The few who choose them are usually those who, granted their temperaments, could not have served society in any better way. And as Mr. Dobie says, a true democracy would recognize that fact. Even most of those who know that, for themselves, some contact with a biosphere means greater health, happiness and content would not deny that what they desire is not to renounce civilization but to enjoy its intellectual and emotional developments without becoming completely a prisoner of its machinery. Even Thoreau who had, or thought he had, so much sympathy with aboriginal wildness often realized that it was not really the life he wanted to lead. "Decayed literature," he wrote, "makes the richest of all soils."

Considered as absolute goods, solitude and freedom from the shrieks and clatters of a mechanized civilization raise the same kind of questions as are raised by "Life in nature." Few men want to be most of the time alone and this is surely their good fortune since most are probably destined to be so less and less often. The only question still worth asking in a civilization like ours which has committed itself to artificial living in a crowded environment is the question of whether or not solitude and quietness are important *as elements;* whether or not at least the opportunity to experience them occasionally as part of a vacation or, in the literal sense of the word, a re-creation, is important. Does to experience them even occasionally provoke thoughts and suggest values not only significant in themselves but likely to provide critical insights into civilization which may influence favorably the course it takes?

How such questions are answered will depend in part upon what one believes about the nature of man as well as upon what satisfaction one, as an individual, happens to take in solitude, quietness, or the spectacle of nature. How fundamental, how nearly unchangeable, is that desire for all these things? Have those who no longer seem to desire them advanced farther along the road to the future than those who do? Are they merely "better adjusted"? Or are they, by just that much less, whole men? Even on the rash assumption that someday mankind will have no contact with anything outside the noosphere, it may still be true that human nature cannot be remade as quickly as his environment can and that he will still, for a long time, suffer a sort of nostalgia for the universe he so long inhabited.

Albert Einstein once told the students at the California Institute of Technology that he doubted whether present-day Americans were any happier than the Indians who were inhabiting the continent when the white man first came. Not many are likely to agree with so extreme a statement but quite a few, I think, would admit that, leaving the Indians out of it, we are not *as much* happier than our grandfathers as it would seem our gains in health, security, comfort, convenience, as well as our release from physical pain ought to make us. Does this failure to pay off have something to do with a misjudgment concerning what man really wants most or, at least, a failure to take into account certain of the things he wants besides comfort, wealth and the rest?

Only more of the same is promised him by even the most optimistic utopians. The more intellectual among them talk in general terms of greater per capita wealth, of less poverty and less manual work, and of faster means of communication. Those who write the popular articles published over and over again in those periodicals which exist chiefly to make readers dissatisfied with their current refrigerator or automobile usually go into more detail. By 1980, they say, you will be broiling steaks in electronic stoves, owning a two-helicopter garage and, of course, looking at television in full color. These assurances are supposed to make it easier for the housewife to put up with mere electric ovens, ninety-mile-an-hour automobiles and soap operas in black and white. From such makeshifts they are supposed to lift sparkling eyes toward a happier future. And perhaps that is precisely what they do do. But will they be as much happier as they now think they inevitably must be? Is it really what they want? Is the lack of these things soon to come chiefly responsible for the irritations, frustrations and discontents they now feel?

Suppose they were promised instead that by 1980 the world in which they live will be less crowded, less noisy, less hurried and, even, less complicated. Suppose they were told that they will have more opportunities to see the beauties and to taste the pleasures of sea and mountain and stream, to have more contact with the wonders of trees and flowers, the abounding life of animal creatures other than human. Would the prospect look even brighter? Perhaps not. But that does not convince me that such a world would not, in actual fact, make for more happiness than the one they are promised.

A true democracy will, as Mr. Dobie said, have some consideration for the minority which wants what contact with nature it can get. Perhaps it will consider also the possibility that a larger minority would be the better for the opportunities it wants without always knowing that it wants them—as thousands are discovering every year on a first visit to one of the national parks.

The decision whether they and the wilderness areas are worth having is one that must be made anew. It was made once a generation ago when the Park System was established with the explicit statement that the areas set aside were to be *permanently* reserved for specific purposes—not just preserved until some other use could be found for them. The Dinosaur Canyon project was a deliberate challenge and (as some of its proponents explicitly stated) an attempt to establish a precedent. The attempt was frustrated; but similar attempts directed elsewhere will be made again. If the original intention is now reaffirmed, the parks, monuments and wilderness areas may remain to refresh, educate and inspire for an indefinite number of generations to come.

What men? What needs?

The discovery of America meant different things to different people. To some it meant only gold and the possibility of other plunder. To others less mean-spirited it meant a wilderness which might in time become another Europe. But there were also not a few whose imaginations were most profoundly stirred by what it *was* rather than by what it might become.

The wilderness and the idea of the wilderness is one of the permanent homes of the human spirit. Here, as many realized, had been miraculously preserved until the time when civilization could appreciate it, the richness and variety of a natural world which had disappeared unnoticed and little by little from Europe. America was a dream of something long past which had suddenly become a reality. It was what Thoreau called the great "poem" before many of its fairest pages had been ripped out and thrown away. The desire to experience that reality rather than to destroy it drew to our shores some of the best who have ever come to them.

That most of it is no longer a wilderness is no cause for regret. But it is a cause for congratulation that the four centuries and more which have passed since Columbus set sail have not been long enough to permit men to take over the whole continent as completely as they long ago took over Europe. And that fact is responsible for an important part of the difference which still exists, spiritually as well as physically, between the Old World and the New. The frontier, so long an important influence on the temper of the American, no longer exists. But as James Fisher realized with surprised delight, the continent can still boast a spaciousness, a grandeur, a richness and a variety which a European can hardly imagine until he has seen it.

These are things which other nations can never recover. Should we lose them, we could not recover them either. The generation now living may very well be that which will make the irrevocable decision whether or not America will continue to be for centuries to come the one great nation which had the foresight to preserve an important part of its heritage. If we do not preserve it, then we shall have diminished by just that much the unique privilege of being an American.

About the Author

Joseph Wood Krutch (1898–1970) lived in the Sonoran Desert in Tucson, Arizona, during the final years of his life. Born in Tennessee, Krutch left to join the staff of *The Nation* as a drama and literary critic. At his country home in Connecticut, Krutch began to publish natural history essays. Ensuing trips to the Southwest convinced him to leave the East. In 1952 he and his wife, Marcelle, moved to Tucson, where he continued his prolific writing.